# Facing Divorce— Again

# Michele Michaels
Foreword by
Erin Thiele

## RestoreMinistries.net

NarrowRoad Publishing House

# Michele Michaels
## *Facing Divorce —Again*

Published by:
NarrowRoad Publishing House
POB 830
Ozark, MO 65721 U.S.A.

The materials from Restore Ministries were written for the sole purpose of encouraging women. For more information, visit us at:

**EncouragingWomen.org**
**RestoreMinistries.net**

Unless otherwise indicated, most Scripture verses are taken from the *New American Standard Bible* (NASB). Scripture quotations marked KJV are taken from the *King James Version* of the Bible, and Scripture quotations marked NIV are taken from the *New International Version*. Our ministry is not partial to any particular version of the Bible but **loves** them all so that we are able to help every woman in any denomination who needs encouragement and who has a desire to gain greater intimacy with her Savior.

Cover Design by Tara Thiele

First Printing: 2014

ISBN: 1-931800-50-2
ISBN13: 978-1-931800-50-1
Library of Congress Control Number: 2019905341

# Contents

# Foreword

It's both exciting and rewarding to see this book finally becoming a reality. Michele and I have had a long lovely friendship for years soon after she helped me with editing and proofing our RMI books. Our working relationship developed into a true admiration for Michele, which now has led to the honor of writing the forward to her first Real Life Novel.

You'll notice that we have given Michele permission to use portions of other RMI books and also testimonies submitted and sent to RMI. These confirm what Michele is saying that I'm certain will both motivate and encourage you to seek God for wisdom as she has done and also to make the Lord your most prized and cherished relationship as she exhibits throughout this amazing book.

Don't read this book just once, make sure it's your go to when facing any litigation to stay moving along that narrow path that leads to live—the abundant life He died to give us.

*Erin Thiele*
Restore Ministries International

# Chapter 1

# God is Looking to Reward You

*"And without faith it is impossible to please Him,*
*For he who comes to God must believe that He is*
*And that **He is a rewarder of those who seek Him**."*
*—Hebrews 11:6*

You may have gotten this book for a friend, for a family member, or for yourself, but whomever it is who is facing divorce—they are probably just as shocked or surprised as I was—even if this is the second or third time a divorce was filed against them.

No one can honestly say that when they married that divorce was something that entered into their mind, at least not seriously. So when it does happen, we all are a bit shaken and can't help but think "Not me" or "Not her" "Not him" or "Not them" even though divorce is rampant in our society.

For each one of you who has been hit with divorce, this book is written just for you. God had you in mind from the very moment that I began typing, and He has you on His mind still. If you take nothing else away from this book, please be sure to take this: He is not angry with you, He is not disappointed in you, and He does not think you are a failure. If this is the way you are feeling, or the way someone has spoken to you—it's not from God. I promise.

*"If anyone fiercely assails you **it will not be from Me**. Whoever assails you will fall because of you" (Isa. 54:15).*

His timing and purpose in my life (and in yours), is well beyond what we are able to comprehend. His ways clearly are higher than our ways!

"'For My thoughts are not your thoughts, nor are your ways My ways,' declares the LORD. 'For as the heavens are higher than the earth, so are My ways higher than your ways and My thoughts than your thoughts'" (Isa. 55:8–9).

Though this may not have been *your* idea or *your* plan, trust that the Lord has it in complete control even though you feel someone else may be—like your spouse, the "enemy" or the other woman or other man in your spouse's life. But God says differently... "The **mind** of **man** plans his way, but the LORD **directs** his steps" (Prov. 16:9).

When my husband came into our bedroom to "talk" to me, this time, to tell me he was on his way that afternoon to file for divorce, again, he said that he was leaving me and planned to "find" someone else to marry (though he was already involved with his high school sweetheart). I was able to *quickly* apply each and every principle you are about to read. Even though I had no clue to what was happening right under my nose, God knew and was ready to help me. The same is true for you and your situation!

That's why you are now holding this book, God wasn't shocked or surprise by your divorce either. He knew about it and was way ahead of you. He led me to write this book to give you the help, encouragement, and tell you about His love that you need—right now.

What He decided to do, just to help you, was to send me on ahead. He knew that some of it might be a bit frightening for you, some of the way may seem a bit too narrow, too steep or the chasm a bit too wide, so He sent me on ahead to build a bridge for you.

## The Bridge Builder
### by Will Allen Dromgoole

An old man, going a lone highway,
Came, at the evening, cold and gray,
To a chasm, vast, and deep, and wide,
Through which was flowing a sullen tide.
The old man crossed in the twilight dim;
The sullen stream had no fears for him;
But he turned, when safe on the other side,
have crossed the chasm, deep and wide -
Why build you the bridge at the eventide?"

The builder lifted his old gray head:
"Good friend, in the path I have come," he said,
"And built a bridge to span the tide.
"Old man," said a fellow pilgrim, near,
"You are wasting strength with building here;
Y*our* journey will end with the ending day;
You never again must pass this way;
You There followeth after me today
A youth, whose feet must pass this way.
This chasm, that has been naught to me,
To that fair-haired youth may a pitfall be.
He, too, must cross in the twilight dim;
Good friend, I am building the bridge for *him*."

So now there is no more need to worry, fret, or even for you to feel badly about what's up ahead. He told me to tell you that your future looks bright!

*"'For I know the **plans** that I have for you,' declares the LORD, 'plans for welfare [wellbeing, happiness, goodness, and safety] and not for calamity to give you a **future** and a hope'" (Jer. 29:11).*

It may not look like this right now, and it certainly may not feel like it, but will you trust someone who has just come through it and is happier than ever?

No, I don't believe in divorce. I would never (not in a million years) choose divorce for my children or for myself—but maybe like you, you had no choice in the matter. When that day did hit, I made a decision that I would like you to make. My decision was to walk *through* it as a TRUE believer. If I could trust God for my eternity, the moment that I died, then couldn't I trust Him with here and now? What about you?

So I chose to walk *through* it **this time** without fear, and without taking the tiny baby steps that I took last time because way back then I had thought that at any moment I was about to fall off a cliff!

This time I knew that God was calling me to not just *apply* the principles I learned and lived the first time around—this time I was going to follow them *enthusiastically*—and the results were astounding!

Not only did they work, but they worked in direct proportion to how *enthusiastically* I applied them! Within 24 hours of responding to my husband's plan (of leaving me and filing for divorce) *enthusiastically*, my husband's heart instantly turned back to me and he dropped the divorced, but that's not all. He went on to **praised me** for the incredible wife I was, and told me he would be a fool to leave me!

However, if it had ended there, where would you be? Miracles do happen, but for most of us, God calls us to walk *through* those valleys that feel like death—doesn't He?

"Even though I walk *through* the valley of the shadow of death, I fear no evil, for You are with me" (Psalm 23:4).

God had a bigger plan for my life (and yours) so He has chosen me to experience the reality of divorce in order to help you. God's plan may be to stop **your** divorce, or He may be calling you to go *through* it so you can help at least one other man or woman—are you willing to trust Him?

Even though my husband's heart wanted to stay with me (and our children), he had fallen into the deep pit of adultery, once again.

"For the harlot is a deep pit, and an adulterous woman is a narrow well. She lurks as a *robber,* and *increases the faithless* among man" (Prov. 23:28).

Even though he wanted out of his plan, very soon the "cords that had him bound" pulled him back—so sad. "His own iniquities will capture the wicked, and he will be held with the cords of his sin" (Prov. 5:22). So, as you walk through this keep this in mind… things will look or appear strange because there is a spiritual battler going on that you cannot see. If your spouse is involved with someone else, he or she may want to be with you, but just like every sin: like drugs or drinking; though they may hate it and want out, they are held by the cords of their sin.

So, though he wanted to stay with me, he was already in too deep, so very soon the divorce pursuit was back on, but that's what the Bible says so I knew it was going to happen.

"But each one is tempted when he is carried away and enticed by his own lust. Then when lust has conceived, it gives birth to sin; and when sin is accomplished, it brings forth death" (James1: 14–15).

When divorce or any other tragedy happens, do you know that God has a much greater purpose? "That when the wicked sprouted up like grass and all who did iniquity flourished, it was only that they might be **destroyed forevermore**" (Psalm 92:7).

## Knowing God's Principles

All the verses that I have shared with you so far are just the beginning of the principles that I want to share with you in this book. These principles are the truths that have set me free! Set me free from worry, from pain, and have led me toward the abundant life that Jesus died to give each of us who are willing to trust Him.

One of the greatest components to my being able to follow the principles "enthusiastically" (my voice was excited, happy, without fearful trepidation that I had the first time my husband divorced me), was because of the testimonies from other women that I had been compiling for this book—two in particular helped me tremendously. They were from women who shared how the Lord had given them the faith to actually "sign" the divorce papers when their husbands asked.

Although one shared how her hand was shaking in the attorney's office, and that tears welled up in her eyes, it was because of *her* faith that I was able to go and sign my divorce papers without my hands trembling (even a little) and with a smile on my face because I had joy in my heart!

*"And they overcame him because of the blood of the Lamb and because of the **word of their testimony,** and they did not love their life even when faced with death" (Rev. 12:11).*

So many women wonder why I had to go through divorce again. I believe it's because the Lord wanted me to learn and experience divorce once again just to help you! The first time I went through divorce I was in incredible pain due only to so much fear!

You must believe this… God knew that on this very day that you would be facing divorce and He wanted you to have the faith, the principles, the knowledge, the understanding, and the courage to face it enthusiastically since He has a wonderful plan for your life!!

"But just as it is written, 'THINGS WHICH **EYE** HAS NOT **SEEN** AND **EAR** HAS NOT HEARD, AND which HAVE NOT ENTERED THE HEART OF MAN, ALL THAT GOD HAS PREPARED FOR THOSE WHO LOVE HIM'" (1 Cor. 2:9).

If you embrace His principles and the love He has for you, then you, too, will be a "walking testimony" of His love and His power when facing any foe, trial, or tribulation because of your facing divorce testimony!

Right up front let me tell you that God does have a plan for your life.

"'For I know the plans that I have for you,' declares the LORD, 'plans for welfare and not for calamity to give you a future and a hope'" (Jeremiah 29:11).

These verses tell us that His plan if for good things, not for calamity or disaster as some love to tell you. So wonderful are His plans for you that He says… neither your eye has seen, nor your ear has heard, not even anything that you could have hidden in your heart is as **great** as what He has prepared for you if you love Him!

This is so true: I cannot begin to tell you of the unbelievable turn of events due solely to trusting God and doing it enthusiastically because I really believed this one principle. I believed He had a plan for my life, therefore, I could run toward it without fear.

## He'll Give You a Choice

The first time I faced divorce the Lord restored my marriage because that was the desire of my heart back then. I truly believed that my heart would no longer be broken if my husband just came back home and my marriage was restored, which was causing me unbearable pain, and that is why you are pursuing restoration too, I'm sure.

But, because I had no fear of my future, I was able to follow the Lord's principles faster, and enthusiastically (as I said); therefore, this time my husband's heart turned back even quicker (as I also shared). But that was not the end of it. AFTER our divorce was final, my ex-husband asked me to marry him again! God had given me a choice.

My choice was, once again, based on the desires of my heart (since I have delighted myself in Him again). This time the Lord won! Both of the men in my life (Jesus and my ex-husband) were alluring and speaking kindly to me. However, as I told my husband when he proposed, who could compete with a Husband like I have now!

"My beloved is mine, and I am His… When I found Him whom my soul loves; I held on to Him and *would not let **Him** go*…For I am lovesick." (Song of Solomon 3:2–4; 5:8).

Dear reader, the choice will also be yours. Don't think that just because I chose to remain single you will end up that way too if you follow the principles *enthusiastically* or fall in love with your Beloved, Jesus, as I have. Like Paul I don't want to put any pressure on you, but instead I just want you to find (as I did) the abundant life that the Lord died to give you. And that abundant life should start **now**!!

"The woman who is unmarried, and the virgin, is concerned about the things of the Lord, that she may be holy both in body and spirit; but one who is married is concerned about the things of the world, how she may please her husband. This I say for your own benefit;

not to put a restraint upon you, but to promote what is appropriate and to secure undistracted devotion to the Lord" (1 Cor. 7:34–35). And as for men, verse 32–34, "But I want you to be free from concern. One who is unmarried is concerned about the things of the Lord, how he may please the Lord, but one who is married is concerned about the things of the world, how he may please his wife, and his interests are divided."

Believe it or not, facing divorce *enthusiastically* will not only turn your husband's or wife's heart back to you (though he/she may have to remain caught in the sin until he/she hates it), but this kind of powerful reaction when your husband or wife files or proceeds through with the divorce, will turn out to be one of the greatest and most *joyful* experiences that you will experience!

How? Why? Because this just may be the closest to the Savior that you have ever been! And with this amount of intimacy with the Lord, your heart just feels like it will burst due to never experiencing this kind of joy—your heart is overflowing with excitement.

Is there absolutely no pain? Truthfully, there was honestly **no** pain this time; just a tiny pinch and the pinch actually had a sense of "sweetness" to it. Not only that, but the tears that I shed this time were also very different, since they came come from a heart who was grateful for the presence and love of the Lord, not tears shed from pain or loneliness like the first time.

It is my hope and prayer that my testimony and this book will encourage you to go beyond the level of faith that I gained from Vivian in Singapore, who signed her papers. I believe that if you embrace the truth in this book (the principles and the testimonies) that you will be able to go well beyond what either of us have gone in order to give God even greater glory! Vivian and I love to share how blessed our lives are now, due to our trusting the Lord.

Even more that what you will learn in this book, you must first focus on developing a close and intimate relationship with the Lord. This can only happen when you begin to spend more and more time with Him. It was in my prayer closet that I was comforted, and gained the strength
to face what I faced the year of my divorce, just yesterday, what I am facing today, and what I will be facing tomorrow.

Fasting also played a tremendous role in my victory over my "self." It enabled me to be quiet and not comment when my flesh could have said "something." Instead it was the *silence* that really brought the victory in each battle I faced. When I added fasting, as the Lord prompted me, I found it brought even greater joy, greater peace, and greater victory to each trial I faced.

Be sure that along with knowing, meditating, and studying these principles, that you apply them *after* you develop and foster deep intimacy with your Lord—who is now your Husband and you are His bride if you are a woman. And for you men, well, I am not sure how to describe the feels you will have, but no doubt, they will be just as wonderful. Now, listen to this…

"'Do not be afraid; you will not suffer shame. Do not fear disgrace; you will not be humiliated. You will forget the shame of your youth and remember no more the reproach of your widowhood. For your Maker is your Husband—the LORD Almighty is his name—the Holy One of Israel is your Redeemer; he is called the God of all the earth. For the LORD has called you, like a wife forsaken and grieved in spirit, even like a wife of one's youth when she is rejected,' Says your God" (Isa. 54:4-6).

The victory is not that a divorce **may** *be* stopped, since very often it takes a husband or wife going *through* the divorce to really see what he or she threw away (especially with the new man or woman you are becoming!). It's not just in a restored marriage (as it happened with the other women who signed their papers in faith or what happened to me the first time around). Victory is living His plan for your life—the abundant life He died to give you.

Daily we fight our flesh that wants its own way and cries out to be fed (by doing what we want to do). We fight the enemy who is working tirelessly to steal our testimony, our joy, and our miracle. In the book of Revelation, it tells us that the enemy literally sits at the birthing stool to kill the miracle when God delivers it.

*". . . and she was with child; and she cried out, being in labor and in pain to give birth . . . And the dragon stood before the woman who was about to give birth, so that when she gave birth he might devour her child" (Rev. 12:2, 4).*

*"Shall I bring to the point of birth and not give delivery?' says the LORD. Or shall I who gives delivery shut the womb?' says your God" (Is. 66:9).*

Please do not wait to read this book all the way through or wait to give it to your friend. Even if your husband or wife has never mentioned the word "divorce," we have to face the fact that one out of every two marriages end in divorce! I had **no idea** that my husband would walk in and tell me he was divorcing me the day he did! This utter surprise or shock is the same reaction most everyone experiences too. The fact that you are reading this book right now tells me (and it should tell you) that it *may* be about to happen in your life, or in the life of someone who is very close to you.

This book was given to you by God to get you ready for what is up ahead so that you can ***benefit, yes benefit,*** from facing divorce rather than be destroyed by it! "A thousand may fall at your side, and ten thousand at your right hand, but **it shall not approach you**" (Ps. 91:7).

Without the wisdom, the principles, and the testimonies that God had me gather together *just for you*, destruction and devastation would certainly happen as it does in most cases of divorce. But with these principles, along with the deep intimacy that you will experience with the Lord (and fasting as you are prompted by the Holy Spirit)— I promise that you will suffer **no** harm!

In fact, you are about to ***prosper*** right in the midst of it all—just as I am doing right now! On the very day that my divorce was to be final I knew that God allowed it, because He LOVES me! He allowed it in order to *prosper* me, and He allowed it in order to give me an awesome *future*!

"I know what I'm doing. I have it all planned out—plans to take care of
you, not abandon you, plans to give you the *future* you hope for" (Jer. 29:11 Message Bible).

If you choose to focus on this truth, rather than what you have been focusing on, destruction, you, too, will obtain all that God has set aside just for you! However, if you instead choose to believe the lies that other people are telling you, or you entertain the fear that the enemy is trying to put in your heart, then I guarantee that you will fall just like all the others you know who faced divorce either with fear or anger. Remember, "A thousand may fall at your side, and ten thousand at your right hand, but **it shall not approach you**" (Ps. 91:7).

It simply takes **faith** and believing what God says in His Word versus what you see or have seen. "Now **faith** is the assurance of things hoped for, the conviction of things *not* **seen**" (Heb. 11:1). "And without **faith** it is **impossible** to **please** Him, for he who comes to God **must** believe that He is and that He is a rewarder of those who seek Him" (Heb. 11:6).

Take it from me, and the other men and women who have allowed us to use their testimonies for this book—if you have faith in God and simply walk through this ordeal with Him *enthusiastically rather than fearfully*, you will experience something only few will ever experience in their life—it is the resurrection power that raised Jesus from the dead! You will literally feel that power flowing through you. Dear reader, you have no earthly idea what God has planned for you. You are about to experience what Lazarus and what Jesus felt when God's resurrecting power raised them from the dead!

For me it was only after my divorce that I began to feel this power, and this power just cannot be described. I will tell you that it is a feeling that I thought could only be felt once I made it to heaven. Marriage, my restoration, and being loved by a man here on earth cannot compare. Resurrection power, which is founded in the Father's love (and is the same love that sent us our Savior), is what gave Jesus the ability to be beaten and to hang on the cross.

If divorce is the cross that God has placed before you, dear reader, then fear not—God has given you the strength and peace to pick it up and carry it. And just as Jesus' death on the cross was only the precursor to His being raised from the dead, you, too will see that God has allowed this to bless you, to prosper you, and to give you a future that you never dreamed could happen to you!

# Chapter 2

# Whose Trust IS the Lord

*Blessed is the man who trusts in the LORD*
*and **whose trust IS the LORD**.*
*—Jeremiah 17:5*

When this book was first written, it was because so many women and men continued to call and write to RMI **desperate** for help when their husband or wife told them he/she was planning to, or had filed for divorce. This book has helped so many people who I knew would continue to contact RMI, usually in a panic, since none of us are ever truly prepared to face divorce from a believer's standpoint—by faith!

Even in the church they treat divorce as a death sentence, something to be feared, or something to "recover" from. However, if you go through it with *enthusiasm* rather than fear, by following these simple principles, I guarantee that you will be a *new* man or woman rather than a broken one.

The more you "renew your mind" by reading the truth in this book, the more you will replace the lies of the world with faith in your Lord. Then, the more faith you have, the more the fear you are experiencing will fade away. And, even better, what will remain will be the "peace that surpasses **all** understanding." And, if you want to experience "*joy* unspeakable and full of glory" then embrace and feed on these truths so that you are able to go through it enthusiastically rather than fearfully with trepidation.

By the way, **never, ever** skip reading the Scripture verses, even if you already know them by heart. The verses will do something wonderful to your spirit. There is a "washing of water with the Word" that will cleanse your mind, soul, and spirit. It will put out the fire of fear and start you on your way to that abundant life. Begin by reading this verse:

*"By wisdom a house is built, and by understanding it is established and by knowledge the rooms are filled with all precious and pleasant riches" (Prov. 24:3–4).*

By reading through this book, I believe, you will gain the wisdom, understanding, and knowledge you will need to do "the right thing" by first releasing **your** attorney, and to stop trying to fight against the divorce based on this powerful principle that Jesus taught us.

*"But I say to you, **do not resist an evil person**; but whoever slaps you on your right cheek, turn the other to him also. If anyone wants to sue you and take your shirt, let him have your coat also. Whoever forces you to go one mile, go with him two" (Matt. 5:38–40).*

How can you do that? Simply...

"Trust in the LORD with all your heart, and do not lean on your own understanding. In all your ways acknowledge Him, and He will make your paths straight" (Prov. 3:5–6).

The wisdom gained by reading this book, **especially** the Scripture verses, will help you to know "what" to do, but the only way to gain understanding is to obey what you know is right, which as you read in Matthew 5:38–40 above is to stop resisting!!

Next comes the knowledge, which will help you discern how to handle the next crisis, and how to help guide others who are going through the same or similar crises, since this is why you were called to go through this trial. So many men and or women who focus on themselves, ignoring the people around them who need help, find that they forgo their own restoration since another principle that you need to obey is "Give and it shall be given."

## Release Your Attorney

Releasing your attorney and no longer standing in the way of your spouse's efforts to divorce you, will take faith and trust in the Lord. This faith, I believe, will be gained through reading the **many** awesome testimonies of those who chose to trust in their Lord, and He faithfully "delivered them from **all** their distresses"!

*"Then they cried out to the LORD in their trouble; He delivered them out of their **distresses**" (Ps. 107:6).*

*"Then they cried out to the LORD in their trouble; He delivered them out of their **distresses**" (Ps. 107:13).*

*"Then they cried out to the LORD in their trouble; He delivered them out of their **distresses**" (Ps. 107:19).*

*"Then they cried out to the LORD in their trouble; He delivered them out of their **distresses**" (Ps. 107:28).*

Did you notice that God said this four times?!

**If you want to be blessed you must trust the Lord, wholly and only.** Here is what the Bible says,

*"Thus says the LORD, Cursed is the man who trusts in mankind and makes flesh his strength, and whose heart turns away from the LORD. For he will be like a bush in the desert and will not see when*

*prosperity comes, but will live in stony wastes in the wilderness, a land of salt without inhabitant.*

*"Blessed is the man who trusts in the LORD and whose trust IS the LORD. For he will be like a tree planted by the water, that extends its roots by a stream and will not fear WHEN the heat comes; But its leaves will be green, and it will not be anxious in a year of drought Nor cease to yield fruit" (Jer. 17:5–8).*

I wrote everything I went through in this book is utter **boldness** that came from watching God **deliver** me and so many others I have had the privilege to minister to. Our Lord and Savior delivered all of us from the "lion's mouths" and from the "fiery furnace" as He led us *"through* the valley of the shadow of death" of attorneys, divorce papers, and fear that tried to paralyze us.

When I originally began to write this book, I understood what you are now facing, because I was served my papers at my door by the sheriff (when I lived in a crummy townhouse alone with two little boys). There were *many lies* on my divorce papers (that were *fabricated* by my husband and the OW), and my papers stated an amount of child support that I knew would never meet the needs of a single mom with small children. I also knew that by **not** going to court that I would "lose by default," and I had no one else's testimony to tell me what that would mean when my divorce was final.

And just like you, I too, had to "walk by faith" when everyone, including Christians and pastors, were telling me to "get a good Christian attorney to protect yourself and your small children." And by not doing so, I was told I was being a fool and even "deserved" what was going to happen, because I would not try to protect my own children.

However, this time, years later, God saw fit to have me walk an even greater walk of faith. This time when my husband sued me for divorce, I had six children living at home, and he was determined he would pay *no* child support at all. This time I was asked to take thousands and thousands of dollars of debt that he also refused to help pay. This time the Lord asked me to *enthusiastically* sign the papers agreeing to all this and more because, dear one, He wanted a testimony for you!

*"And they overcame him because of the blood of the Lamb and because of the word of their testimony, and they did not love their life even when faced with death" (Rev. 12:11).*

Because of the testimony that the Lord designed just for you, you don't have to face your divorce with terror or the unknown. I have walked the walk-in order to give you a safe and sure path. Everything that I will share with you in this book is something I have lived through.

Dear friend, our God is **faithful** and more **powerful** than any attorney, or any spouse or friend or any circumstance that may come against you! You will experience the same joy that I experienced through my divorce, if you simply trust Him and open your heart up to His love.

"There is no fear in love; but **perfect love** *casts out fear…*" (1 John 4:18).

And through the many testimonies of the faithful men and women who applied the principles from this book, I promise that if you have just a tiny bit of faith, you can go well beyond just peace—you will experience JOY, just as I am doing this second time around!!

Just keep your eyes on the One who can easily save you from any destruction, but instead wants to bless you. Don't choose to allow **fear** to keep you from the blessings of peace, and joy. Fear is the enemy's way of pushing Christians to do what the enemy **knows** will lead to their destruction. You will never gain your **miracle** if you operate in fear. Trust, faith, and **obedience** to His Word will bring about **victory** in your life and a testimony to share with others!

May the Lord bless you with a **joy unspeakable** as you release your attorney and take the hand of Jesus!

Here's the first testimony:

## All of this Happened for a Reason!!

"My husband had moved out and was living with the OW, a co-worker. He was not happy and felt unwanted in our 20+ years of marriage. Prior to deciding to trust the Lord for my marriage, I had sent him emails quoting Scripture and pointing out his sins and faults. That was the wrong way to handle things! He has since shared with me that it just made him mad and confirmed for him that he had done the right thing by leaving!

After approximately six weeks of separation and moving toward divorce, I realized that divorce did not have to be the answer. That's when a pastor friend across the country referred me to the Restore Ministries website. I immediately ordered their books and read them within a couple of days.

I did not immediately release my attorney. I had a hard time with the thought of dismissing my attorney, but I prayed about it, and within a couple of days I knew that I needed to follow through. Immediately a burden was lifted from me once I released my attorney! Everyone, you have to take that step! My outlook changed immediately!

I knew that God was the only one who could restore our marriage; it was only a matter of days before I began to see changes in myself and would stop to think about what I had done to change. I realized it was not me—it was God working in awesome ways! The changes came after I began to realize the things I had done wrong, prayed for

God to change me, and prayed for God's will for our marriage. I had to turn it all over to God and trust Him completely.

My husband began to notice little changes when he stopped by briefly for the kids or the mail. A mutual friend was also telling him how much I had changed. I asked my husband to forgive me for my contentiousness in the past. Getting past those ways was a relief to me; it is so much better to live a non-contentious life! Life is much more enjoyable, and I am happier, too. Of course, this also comes from having the Spirit of God living within me!

My husband couldn't imagine that the changes were real and that I wasn't putting on a front, trying to get him back for the wrong reasons. We did not talk much but would occasionally email to discuss the kids. Just as Erin mentioned in her book, he tested me at times when he talked to me. I felt this happen on several occasions where he would say something to see if I would react. I did not react, as I would have in the past, which showed him that I was really a new person.

There were several different events coming up over the holidays, and I hoped that we would attend them together as husband and wife. It didn't happen. The kids and I were with my family in a resort area for Christmas, and I had invited my husband, letting him know he could join us at any time during the week. I prayed that he would show up on Christmas—it was the only thing I wanted! I went to bed crying and praying, but also realizing that it would happen in God's timing, not mine. Once I acknowledged to God that He alone could know when we were both ready, that's when restoration happened.

It was December 28, and my husband showed up at the resort. I did not expect it, and my husband didn't know until 30 minutes prior to leaving our hometown for the resort that he would return home! He wasn't sure why he was there, but I assured him it was God who had brought him.

Ladies [and gentlemen], be sure to turn it all over to God. When you are waiting and having a rough day, pray, and pray some more! If it weren't for my faith, for our awesome God, and for prayer, I would not have gotten through! Do not fight in the flesh—it will only frustrate you and slow your restoration. I found that so many things happened just as Erin said they would in the *Restoration* and *Wise Woman* book. I followed her advice, read the Scriptures, and prayed, and that is what got me through. It will get you through also.

"If God brings you to it, He will bring you through it." All of this happened for a reason. God had a plan, and now my husband and I are so much happier. We are living for God, we have a great marriage, and it just gets better every day!

Thank you, Erin, for your ministry. It is so awesome how you have helped so many marriages, ours included! God is wonderful, and what a gift He has given you!

~ *Lydia in Colorado—now RESTORED!*

## Back Together After 19 Months!

This donation comes with praise to God for what He has done! My husband and I are back together after having been separated for 19 months! After we had been separated a year, my husband filed for divorce, stating that there was no way he was ever going to get back together with me.

I had read your books and listened to your tapes and I must say, I was very skeptical about some of the things you had to say—they seemed pretty radical—especially the part about letting my lawyer go. But, during the months of separation from my husband, I clung to God, really pressing in to seek Him with all my heart. God was so faithful to me, carrying me through the incredible trials of separation and provided so completely for everything I needed!

At the time of our separation, I had two small children, ages four and two, and I was three months pregnant with our third child. Also, my husband had cut me off from our bank account, so I had no income. It was incredibly stressful and difficult, but as I look back, it is so amazing to see how God lovingly took care of me through everything I faced. He protected me and brought me to a place of rest in Him.

In February, after 15 months of separation, I finally decided to let my lawyer go. It was completely an act of faith because my husband was extremely hostile toward me. Also, the divorce case was impending, and we had not agreed to any financial or marital settlement. I was trusting in God to provide for me.

I felt incredible pressure from my lawyers not to do what I was doing. I don't think they were purposefully trying to scare me—I'm sure they felt like they were just trying to do their job and look out for my interests—but they gave me very stern warnings that I was leaving myself unprotected and that my husband's lawyer would try to take advantage of me. In spite of the pressure and the fear, I went ahead and let the lawyers go. I told God that I would give Him any money that was returned to me from the legal retainer I had paid.

So—praise be to the Lord!—this money is from the legal retainer. Had it not been for the wisdom I received through your ministry, I might not have ever let my lawyers go (and I would probably have ended up in divorce court). Within a month of my letting them go, my husband pulled his divorce suit! And now, finally, after an incredible journey, my husband has moved in with me and our three children. God has completely turned my husband's heart back to me. Praise God—I cannot praise Him enough!"

~ *Darlene in Virginia—now RESTORED.*

Do you have this kind of faith? Save the money that you would pay an attorney that will destroy your marriage and donate it where you will reap a bountiful harvest by helping restore marriages!

# Chapter 3

# Running Over

*Give, and it will be given to you.*
*They will pour into your lap a good measure—*
*pressed down, shaken together, and **running over**.*
*For by your standard of measure*
*it will be measured to you in return.*
*—Luke 6:38*

## Responding Enthusiastically

One of the most *powerful* and *freeing* attitudes that God worked into my spirit this time during my divorce was to respond "enthusiastically" to *everything* my husband said when he wanted to "talk" to me. Compare this to the first time my husband divorced me— the first time I only had the faith to timidly "agree," and the agreement was coupled with pain, doubt, worry, and much "follow up" prayer once I did agree!

Beloved, this is not the abundant life Jesus died to give us—it is instead the burden that we were never intended to carry! The first time, instead of trusting in the Lord that all would work out for my good (Romans 8:28), that the Lord longed to be gracious to me (Isaiah 30:18), and was actually "waiting" to show Himself strong on my behalf (2 Chronicles 16:9), I would instead spend my time mulling over the consequences of what was being presented or asked of me, which brought about such a heavy burden that I struggled to survive.

What changed? Not the situation. This time around, the attack was much quicker; the demands much greater, the loss would be much more substantial, and the scandal far greater. The difference was in me. I had gained more faith through reading the testimonies submitted to the ministry, I had developed more spiritual strength from walking in obedience, and I was now full of the Holy Spirit, but most importantly, I had a closer and more intimate relationship with the Lord. He was my Husband now, and because of this intimacy, the Lord would continually show me what was "up ahead" so that I would not be caught off guard.

*"Ask Me about the things to come..." (Isa. 45:11). "Your ears will hear a word behind you, 'This is the way, walk in it,' whenever you turn to the right or to the left" (Isaiah 30:21).*

All of these advantages, dear reader, are available to you! This book, and everything the RMI ministry offers will help you learn how to hear and follow the Lord. The key, and what is the most important, is your one-on-one time spent with the Lord. He will give you the ability to not just make it *through*, but help you to prosper, to be blessed, and most importantly to have JOY that enables you to enjoy, not just endure the journey! This may sound impossible to you; I know that had I read this the first time around, I would have thought so too. But it is well within every believer's reach!

"Not that I speak from want; for I have **learned to be content** in *whatever circumstances* I am" (Phil. 4:1). ". . . being **content** with *what you have*; for He Himself has said, 'I will never desert you, nor will I ever forsake you'" (Heb. 13:5). "But *godliness* is actually a means of great gain, when *accompanied* by **contentment**" (1 Tim. 6:6).

When my husband came in to "talk" to me, he said, "I am on my way out the door to speak to an attorney. I am going to divorce you and I plan to find someone else to marry." My response surprised us both, "Oh, okay, I understand," and I smiled!

Because my response was not one of fear, shock, or horror, he was sure that he had not said it clearly enough, so he said it again, and with much more intensity. So, dear reader, if you choose to respond graciously (as you trust the Lord and refuse to stand in the path of the wicked), you need to be prepared for more attacks. The heat will be turned up each and every time your spouse states he/she is leaving you, and he/she will begin to include *why*. But, praise God, my heart had been "hidden in the Lord" for many weeks.

God actually had been preparing me for this moment for almost a year (though I didn't know or suspect it). And believe it or not, He has been preparing you, too, even though you were not aware of it either.

God *promises* that the righteous will **not** be shaken. "Cast your burden upon the LORD and He will sustain you; He will never allow the **righteous** to be **shaken**" (Ps. 55:22). This is His promise to you and me. Therefore, He does His best to show you what is up ahead, and also begins to draw you closer to Him so you will be ready. Right now, in the midst of this mess and this trial, ladies, He is wooing you, and alluring you to come to Him and be His bride. For you gentlemen, He is also there to support and strengthen you.

*"Therefore, behold, I will **allure** her, bring her into the wilderness, and speak kindly to her" (Hos. 2:14).*

In my situation, the Lord began showing me while reading my Bible every morning that my husband would "be gone." He didn't tell me *how* or *why*, just that he would not be there. It kept coming up in so many verses that He would lead me to read every day.

The Lord also began to plant in my heart that the only One I wanted, and the only One I needed was Him! I would say it over, and over, and over again all day—"Lord, you are all I want and all that I need" especially when I laid down at night to go to sleep, and every morning when I woke up. As "evil plans" were "stirring" in the mind of my husband to leave me for another woman, the Lord began to draw me nearer to Him so that I would be safe.

*"Keep me as the apple of the eye; hide me in the shadow of Your wings" (Ps. 17:8).*

The Lord may have been trying to get your attention before your spouse mentioned divorce or before you found out about the other woman or man in your spouse's life. If all of this has taken place, and it has left you *shaken*, it is not too late to begin to be sensitive to the Lord, and the leading of the Holy Spirit. It simply takes making time with Him through: prayer, time in your prayer closet, reading His Word, lots of time thanking and praising Him, but most importantly, just sitting quietly in His presence and feeling His love for you.

*"I have loved you with an **everlasting love**; therefore I have drawn you with lovingkindness" (Jer. 31:3).*

**Prayer** is just talking to God about everything you would normally tell your closest friend. If Jesus is to be first in our lives, He needs to be our very best friend, and He needs to be the One you and I run to when we need to talk, and we need comfort or assurance. Jesus is always excited (even though He already knows what you are going to say) to hear from you, and He is always faithful to help you feel better. When you tell Him about a traumatic or painful thing that has just happened to you—He truly will be Someone who will stick closer than a brother and comfort you more than a mother!

## Abuse

And let me pause a moment to say this, most women who face divorce, and/or adultery, abandonment, etc., also experience many forms of abuse from their husbands. Verbal abuse usually precedes physical abuse. By never opening your mouth in your defense, or worse, by fighting back (or starting an argument) with cruel or cutting words (especially words that humiliate or attack the character of your spouse) or physically throwing the first punch, you can basically stop **all** physical violence that may be coming at you now. However, be prepared—the *verbal* abuse will probably continue.

The remedy to verbal abuse, and when your husband comes in to have a "talk" with you with words that are terrifying and often shocking, is that you need to first keep your mouth closed and just *listen to the **Lord*** who will speak kindly to you in a still small voice. This means no comments, and *no **questions*** to what your husband tells you! Let your husband do all the talking. When he is done, just agree—it's that simple.

This goes for you men too. Just agree!!

### What? No comments, but what if I don't agree?

Let's be honest, *nothing* you say will change anything your spouse has in his/her mind, right? Every spouse who comes to the place of wanting to leave, and file for divorce, has made up his/her mind. And, by trying to stop him/her you will only *increase* their **passion** to complete what he/she has in their mind to do.

*"Do not be in a hurry to **leave him**. Do not join in an evil matter, for he will do whatever he pleases" (Eccl. 8:3).*

And as far as the questions you have—honestly, no questions you ask will ever give you the answers you are looking for! Instead it will result in much more pain, confusion, and every other negative emotion that you don't need to deal with on top of everything else he/she has already said or done.

*"The mind of man plans his way but the Lord directs his steps" (Prov. 16:9).*

You're right, what he/she said, the reasons he/she states make **no sense**—but that it the way of someone caught in adultery.

*"With her many persuasions she entices him; with her flattering lips she seduces him. Suddenly he follows her as an ox goes to the slaughter, or as one in fetters to the discipline of a fool, until an arrow pierces through his liver; as a bird hastens to the snare, So he does not know that it will cost him his life" (Prov. 7:21–23).*

*"The mouth of an adulteress is a **deep pit**; he who is cursed of the LORD will fall into it" (Prov. 22:14).*

Oh, and just as you read in Lydia's testimony, don't make the mistake of quoting Scriptures (like the one you just read) to your spouse. It will only make him/her angrier and more determined to get as far away from you and GOD as he/she can!!

Most men leave due to falling into the pit of adultery. The first time I knew it right away (I caught him in the act) and yet he denied it. The second time he again told me that he was leaving "to find another woman to marry" but then, later, confessed (due to the proof that began to be revealed) that he was again involved, which was why he so boldly and quickly divorced me—to marry her.

If you are not aware of another woman your husband may be involved with, don't try to find out. This is God's way of protecting you. If this is what is going on, in His good time, He will ease you into all truth. However, if you choose to snoop, suspect, or confront your husband, you are in for horrendous pain that has the potential to haunt you **for years!** Knowing what is going on is not God's plan, but it is the enemy's plan to destroy you. Please trust the Lord, and me, by keeping your eyes on the Lord. You are not being naïve or stupid, you are acting in a wise and gracious manner befitting for a child of God.

The reason many women leave their husbands is due to fear and/or feeling unloved. Women are NOT what the media has convinced you, and you are a fool if you believe it. A woman who feels unloved will leave looking for love. Men and women are different, so cast down the lies you have fed on probably all of your life.

The Bible tells men, in this verse, how they have messed up:

"You husbands in the same way, live with your wives in an understanding way, as with someone *weaker*, since she is a woman; and show her honor as a fellow heir of the grace of life, so that your prayers will not be hindered" (1 Pet. 3:7). Each time you treat her hard and harshly you are destroying her and her love for you! Women were given an internal desire for her husband... "Yet your desire will be for your husband" (Genesis 3:16).

But most men foolishly fail to live with their wives in an "understanding way" honoring her, and treating her as the weaker vessel she is, has pushed his wife out of his live, and often into the arms of another man.

Understanding "way" does not mean that you need to understand how she thinks and feels, but in a way where you are mature enough to listen, not suggest or question, or worse, tell her what to do since women just need someone who will listen to how she feels.

# Chapter 4

# How to Deal with "Those Talks"

*"But sanctify Christ as Lord in your hearts,*
*always being ready to make a defense to everyone*
*who asks you to give an account*
*for the hope that is in you,*
*yet with gentleness and reverence"*
*—1 Peter 3:13-15*

Once your spouse leaves from talking to you, or you hang up the phone, *immediately* go to your prayer closet and tell the Lord everything that you are feeling and thinking. If you have wisely not asked questions and resisted what you wanted to say or do, then, you will find that you not only will recover from this horrible blow, but you will be one step closer to restoration.

Once you go and tell the Lord everything, then (and this is very important and something we so often miss), *sit very quietly* and ask the Lord to tell you how He feels and thinks! This is when you will hear the still small voice of the Lord!! You don't want to miss it by running out to go call a friend, or worse, hurry to tell your spouse what you think or how you feel, or to ask him/her questions about what he/she said!

Remember, *"Do not be in a hurry to leave him. Do not join in an evil matter, for **he [she] will do whatever he [she] pleases"** (Eccl. 8:3).*

God wants you to learn to hear His voice, so He can lead you to find your abundant life. He wants to lead you *through* the "valley of the shadow of death." But to do so, we need to quiet our minds and our spirits and just listen. When you have just been stabbed in the heart, your heart is open to hear His voice like no other time. Then once you have learned how to get alone with Him and hear His voice, you will be able to hear Him *without* needing a wounded to the heart— you will soon be able to hear Him clearly in a loud room. But it begins, first, with going to a quiet place, pouring out your heart, and then being quiet so He can pour out His heart into yours!

Usually, with me, He often begins to speak His Word to me, such as in a Bible verse, which comes into my mind and heart. This is why it is so important that you devour reading your Bible and mark (with a colored pencil) the promises He is showing you. Remember that most of your promises are going to be found in Psalms, and later, you'll find special things from Him throughout the Bible, including some of the Old Testament books that very few Christians read. Just let His Holy Spirit lead you. Begin your Bible reading by asking the Lord what He wants to show you each and every day.

God tells us in the Lord's Prayer to ask for "our daily bread"; therefore, He already has spiritual food, designed just for us, each day. Don't make the mistake of not asking or not being spiritually fed every day—especially while facing divorce. Each spiritual meal is not enough for two days. It is also not enough to eat just once in the morning. And just as the experts in our physical health tell us that eating a lot of small meals throughout the day is better for us, as far as spiritual matters, I will tell you that enjoying the Word of God and being in His presence *throughout* the day, will sustain you and nourish you spiritually rather than spending a longer time just once a day.

*"O **taste** and **see** that the LORD is good; how blessed is the man who takes refuge in Him!" (Ps. 34:8).*

Spiritual meals just don't "happen" so be sure to plan out your day to "taste and see that the Lord is good" not just *once* in the morning, but *feast* on His Word and His promises throughout the day. This will keep you in perfect peace rather than fighting or suffering despair.

**Praise** is another area that will take you to the heights of JOY that will transform you, your life, and whatever you are going though now and in the future. If what is up ahead is keeping you from praising God like He should be praised, let your mind "fast forward" to the future that He has planned for you. Don't look at what "may" be up ahead, like what will happen if or when you sign divorce papers, or the fear of running into the other woman at the ball game, or who your husband/wife might be seeing when he/she is not with you—instead look to the future—a future that He has planned just for you!

*"Delight yourself in the LORD; and He will give you the desires of your heart. Commit your way to the LORD, Trust also in Him, and He will do it. He will bring forth your righteousness as the light and your judgment as the noonday.*

*Rest in the LORD and wait patiently for Him; Do not fret because of him who prospers in his way, because of the man who carries out wicked schemes. Cease from anger and forsake wrath; **Do not fret; it leads only to evildoing.** For evildoers will be cut off, but those who wait for the LORD, they will inherit the land" (Ps. 37:4-9).*

Whatever the Lord has promised you—look ahead and focus on that. Then begin to praise Him like you know you will praise Him when (not if) it happens!! Will you dance and sing before the Lord when your miracle arrives? Then show God you believe Him and praise Him **now**! Don't wait, right in the midst of each onslaught of evil or wickedness—rejoice, because you are now one step closer to the desires of your heart!

When the Israelites took Jericho, they shouted for victory that crumbled the walls! They didn't shout *after* the walls fell down— it was their shout *before*hand that crumbled the walls! And again, in Second Chronicles chapter 20, Jehoshaphat praised God and the Levites stood up to praise the Lord with a very loud voice *before* the victory that caused the enemy to destroy themselves!!! And if that were not enough, after the enemy was completely destroyed, it took them three days to collect all the spoil left behind!! Believe this for your situation since God also promises us for all the injustices done to us.

"Speak kindly to Jerusalem; and call out to her, that her warfare has ended, that her iniquity has been removed, that she has **received** of the LORD'S hand **double** for all her sins" (Isa. 40:2). Did you notice that He said you *will* receive double, not for what you did that was right, but also for what you did wrong? Remember that when you try to beat yourself up with your mistakes. He also said He will give you double for things done to you! Read it…

*"Instead of your shame you will have a **double** portion, and instead of humiliation they will shout for joy over their portion. Therefore they will possess a **double** portion in their land, everlasting joy will be theirs" (Isa. 61:7).*

**It is what you *believe* that is the deciding factor between prospering and destruction.**

*"Truly I say to you, whoever says to this mountain, 'Be taken up and cast into the sea,' and does not doubt in his heart, but believes that what he says is going to happen, it will be granted him" (Mark 11:23).*

If you believe that destruction is up ahead, it surely will happen. If, however, you believe that God is a good God, and is using this crisis to bless you (and bless you each and every step of the way), then that is what will happen.

Be sure to focus on what God has done for you rather than what may be coming against you! Each day, as the song says, "Count your blessings, name them one by one; count your blessings, see what God has done!" Do this as you lay down to go to bed at night, and again in the morning. Thank Him for each thing He did for you the day before. When you get on the phone to talk to your friend, name your *blessings* one-by-one—stop talking about the bad things. God loves to be praised; therefore, He will continue to bless the ones who will take the time and effort to give Him the praise He deserves!!

**Praise the Lord in song.** Sing songs that sing *to* Him not *about* Him; songs that speak to the Lord, in the first person. It is very easy to find great praise and worship music—praise the Lord—it's everywhere! You might be drawn to what your church sings, but also try also to branch out by asking your friends (who are on-fire for the Lord) what they listen to. I am pleased to have sons who play on the Praise and Worship team in their church. So, since they are often practicing, their praise and worship music is what I hear *continually* and what I tend to prefer.

Not only is praise music a way to turn your mourning into dancing, but so do love songs that you sing **to** the Lord. There are lots of Christian *love* songs that you might hear at weddings. These songs used to pierce my heart because, like Leah from the Bible, I never felt truly loved by my husband. (Men, are you listening? Because I will tell you that is why your wife has left you.) But ever since I began singing *love* songs to the Lord, I feel I am the most blessed and loved woman on this earth! I am truly HIS bride.

Once you are done praising the Lord in song and dance, and you've sung that special *love* song to Him, make sure you also tell Him how you feel about Him. Tell Him how much you love Him. Tell Him that there is no one and nothing you want or need besides Him. This kind of interaction needs to be done all day long— whenever you experience any negative feelings, and each time you experience good things that happen to you. Just make sure you take the time to tell Him how much you love Him and cherish Him.

This kind of interaction with the Lord will prepare you for any and every "talk" your spouse might approach you with. It will take no real "effort" on your part to simply *just agree*, but to respond to what he/she says ***enthusiastically***!! Because, your trust is in the Lord not the plans the enemy is trying to make happen, and when I say "enemy" I am not talking about the plans your spouse or the other person in their lives may have to destroy you but who is behind it. Remember they are in the process of having their lives destroyed too—they just don't realize it!

So, instead of fretting, you will join in with the Lord as He laughs at what the enemy is trying to do because His Word says…

"Why are the nations in an uproar and the peoples devising a vain thing? The kings of the earth take their stand and the rulers take counsel together Against the LORD and against His Anointed... He who sits in the heavens laughs, the Lord scoffs [makes fun] at them" (Psalm 2: 1–4).

Through the power I have gained through a close of intimacy with the Lord, coupled with being baptized in the Holy Spirit (which automatically gives you spiritual boldness), which I did not have the first time around, along with the testimonies that I began to read to gather for this book, I was able to not just agree (or endure), but I could respond to all my husband's evil plans *enthusiastically*. This is because I knew that everything that happened and everything that looked negative would eventually turn out to be a blessing for me (and my children)!

*"We know that God causes all things to work together for good to those who **love God**, to those who are called according to **His purpose**" (Rom. 8:28).*

I was able to: *enthusiastically* take on all of our family and business debt (and there was ten times what I thought we had!), *enthusiastically* sign the divorce papers so that my husband would **not** have to pay any child support and *enthusiastically* listened to my husband telling me more and more about the woman he was involved with.

*"Who will **separate** us from the **love** of Christ? Will tribulation, or distress, or persecution, or famine, or nakedness, or peril, or sword?" (Rom. 8:35).*

*"My beloved is mine, and I am His... When I found Him whom my soul loves; I held on to Him and would not let him go...**For I am lovesick**." (Song of Solomon 3:2–4; 5:8).*

**\*When Jesus is all you need and all you want—no one can hurt you.**

As a result, now I not only have peace, but I have **joy** that makes me want to leap and dance. But that is far from all, the Lord has gone before me and surrounded me with favor everywhere I turn! Opportunities have come up that I never dreamed would happen to me, as well as financial blessings that turn up each and every day!

This is not just available to me, but to each and every one of you who chooses this path Jesus encouraged us to take— rather than the wide and destructive road that the world takes when facing divorce.

*"In everything, therefore, treat people the same way you want them to treat you, for this is the Law and the Prophets. Enter through the narrow gate; for the gate is wide and the way is broad that leads to destruction, and there are many who enter through it. For the gate*

*is small and the way is narrow that leads to life, and there are few who find it" (Matt. 7:12–14).*

Sadly, the wide road to destruction is the very same road that most Christians choose to take right beside the unbeliever. Foolishly they take the same path as the unbeliever by retaining a "good" attorney to *fight* for them and by trying to block and fight the evil when Jesus told us clearly **not** to!

*"But I say to you, **do not resist an evil person**; but whoever slaps you on your right cheek, turn the other to him also. If anyone wants to sue you and take your shirt, let him have your coat also. Whoever forces you to go one mile, go with him two" (Matt. 5:38–40).*

Some Christians may not be able to achieve this "holy" boldness, because they have not been filled with the Holy Spirit. And by the way, holy boldness is not the "in-your-face" kind of attitude; it is instead the ability to turn the other cheek and to remain quiet when being accused unjustly.

*"For you have been called for this purpose, since Christ also suffered for you, leaving you an example for you to follow in His steps . . . and while being reviled, **He did not revile in return;** while suffering, **He uttered no threats,** but kept entrusting Himself to Him (God) who judges righteously" (1 Pet. 2:21-23).*

What does it mean to be filled, or baptized in the Holy Spirit? It is to get more of God. I know without a doubt, that this one asset I had this time, which gave me the spirit boldness and spiritual fuel that I needed to be able to "benefit" rather than simply "endure" this spiritual onslaught of the wicked against me (and my children) that meant that I did not need to struggle.

Being filled with the Holy Spirit is a gift, which means you can't earn it or work for it—just like your salvation is a gift. It's just something you ask for and trust that you will receive it. To gain an understanding of this gift, read the book of Acts 2 and Acts 4. Also, listen to the "Be Encouraged" videos, which also explains this gift that Jesus told the disciples to wait for.

If Jesus told the apostles (who were hiding in the upper room after the crucifixion) to wait there until they got filled with the Holy Spirit, then it is something that you, too, should desire to have no matter what your denominational beliefs. I want all God has for me, how about you?

# ———— Chapter 5 ————

# Beyond Agreement

*"If anyone wants to sue you and take your shirt,*
*give him your coat also."*
*—Matthew 5:40*

During my first divorce the Lord helped me to learn how to "agree with my adversary" (Matthew 5:25 KJV), but this time He chose to bring me (and you) higher. Going higher with God means greater intimacy, greater blessings, and to get there—greater tests and deeper trials.

The principle that I learned to use this time says, "But I say to you, *do **not** resist* an evil person; but whoever slaps you on your right cheek, turn the other to him also. If anyone wants to sue you and take your shirt, let him have your coat also. Whoever forces you to go one mile, go with him two. Give to him who asks of you, and do not turn away from him who wants to borrow from you" (Matthew 5:39–42).

This one principle has always yielded huge blessings in my life, but none so much as when I was facing divorce this time. This principle of going ***beyond*** what is asked of us, coupled with doing it "enthusiastically," will yield blessings that you never dreamed of— just as it has done for me!

Though it was God who began leading me to do this, once I was able to consciously looking for opportunities, I took a moment one day to go to my prayer closet to make sure that I totally and completely understood **when** to apply this principle of giving *beyond* what was asked: to go the second mile, to give the coat when only asked for the shirt, to turn to the other cheek.

The Lord's answer was so simple; He said it is when they **ask**! Well, duh, it does say that, doesn't it??!! But sometimes the simplest things evade our ability to comprehend them.

It was each time my husband "asked" for something when I was supposed to *give* him **more** than he asked for. And the awesome thing is that when you and I are walking in the Spirit of the Lord, are yielded to His will, and are sensitive to Him because we have spent lots of time with Him, we don't even have to stop and think of what to give *beyond* what is asked, it just rolls right off our tongue!!

Most Christians instead resist what is asked of them, or give it *finally* in a bargain, with strings attached! Is it any wonder why Christian marriages collapse at a higher rate than the unbeliever? It is time for believers to live according to the example the Lord left us to follow, and to take the power of the Holy Spirit, and follow what He said we are supposed to do!

In the process of revising this book my husband told me he was going to move away and asked if he could take our younger children with him (or fly them there) periodically for a week or two since they are homeschooled. I responded *enthusiastically* "of course!" and then went on to say without having to think about it, "I have a friend up there that I would love to meet, so whenever you like, I can drive them up myself and then drive them back, saving you some time and money!"

My husband was so grateful, and then tender towards me for many days later. I was not trying to allure my husband, because I am not seeking restoration (this time I am only interested in pursuing the Lord); nevertheless, I can see that though I am not interested, following these principles act like a *magnet* since this is humility! No one can resist kindness shown to them, especially when they are "undeserving" of it and when there are no strings attached. Though they may try to resist, humility begins to penetrate a hardened heart and causes a spouse to begin to see the difference between who he/she might be pursing and the one he/she is choosing to leave behind. Are you listening?

[Side note: since writing this it has been three years and I never once was asked to drive my children ten hours north! Instead, because I followed these principles, enthusiastically, not allowing fear or reason to stop me from following the principles I am sharing with you now, the Lord actually blessed me! Because in the divorce papers it clearly states that each of us is responsible to *share* the delivery or retrieval of the children and that has never once been asked of me! This, dear reader, is God at work!]

Also, being uninterested in your spouse who has left you, or filed for divorce is extremely alluring (especially when you don't want it to be, since it is so sincere). So many men/women refuse to let go of their spouse, and as result, are caught in an endless cycle of pain. If you make Jesus all you want and all you need then your heart will rest safely in His hands and the desire to get your spouse back will fade in your attitude. This will result in your spouse alluring/pursing you! How's that for a turn of events?

It will **not** work, however, but will backfire, if you are playing games. Many people will tell you to *pretend* you are involved with someone else or something stupid like that. Playing games is also deceptive, and God will not be mocked.

When you are involved with Jesus, I guarantee that you will look as if you have a Lover, and you will glow. Couple that will *enthusiastically* letting go, and the tables will turn more quickly than the weeks, months, or years it took for your spouse to want nothing to do with you!! Guaranteed!!

# Chapter 6

# I Declare New Things

*"Behold, the former things have come to pass,*
*Now I declare new things;*
*Before they spring forth I proclaim them to you."*
—Isaiah 42:8–9

*"I am the LORD, and there is no other, the One forming light and creating darkness, causing well-being and creating calamity; I am the LORD who does all these" (Is. 45:6–7).*

*"You will not be put to shame or humiliated to all eternity" (Is. 45:17).*

It was after my husband got back from a trip, that he told me, to my utter surprise, that he was on his way to an appointment with an attorney for a divorce. He said that he still loved me, but he wanted to find someone who was more compatible with him. (Later it was revealed that he already had a woman, his girlfriend from high school that he was seeing and had planned, or hoped, to marry.)

However, God told me many months earlier that my husband was "not going to be here" (as I said earlier). I had no idea that he had made a *decision* to leave, and certainly not that he was secretly involved with someone!

It happened in January, before I let go of my church, during a Wednesday prayer meeting. Our pastor told us that the Lord wanted to speak to us about what He had for us that year, and I was excited to find out! So I bowed my head, and the Lord began to speak to me. He told me that 2005 would be the hardest year of my life, but that in 2006, *every* promise He had given me would come to pass. Yes, I shook a bit, and cried a lot that night. But, when we were asked to stand up and sing, the Lord told me to sing and praise Him as if 2006 and all those promises had been fulfilled—I did, and **joy** overflowed from my heart.

However, while I waited for "what was coming," I had all kinds of "vain imaginations" of what "it" might be. I began thinking that my husband might be killed (since I had been called to minister with so many widows all of a sudden), and then that it might mean that he was going to be incarcerated (since RMI began having a lot of members whose husbands were going to jail). Then, a few weeks before "it" hit, the Lord awakened me in the middle of the night. He told me that all these thoughts were just "vain imaginations" and that I needed to "take my thoughts captive."

When "it" did come, I knew I needed to contact the ministry to let everyone know of the turn of events in my marriage since I had a restored marriage and was a RMI minister. Thankfully everyone was more than supportive when shared it with them and encouraged me that He would use it for everyone's good!

Those who had difficulty with what had happened were mostly concerned with what it meant in their own life and marriage. Some women, understandably, thought that it must have meant that somehow, I had failed as a wife or my husband would not have chosen to leave. I knew that I could not and should not defend myself and left it to the Lord to do it for me.

Later many of those who accused me contacted me when the Lord reminded them of Job's friends who were sure that his trials were due to sin in his life.

Initially, when my husband told my children and his family, he placed all the blame on me for the failed marriage and for his *having* to divorce me. Rumors then began to run rampant in my church where we were both leaders. Again, I remained quiet and trusted the Lord for my reputation. God showed up, as He usually does, in the midst of a huge crisis, when our senior pastor came against me (and threatened to shut down my ministry to women within his church). It left me in tears when my husband unexpectedly came in…the result?

My husband got on the phone with our pastor and defended me!! He said that **everything** was *"his"* fault," that I had been "the perfect wife," and he (my pastor) should know what kind of a person I was!!! Yes, this is God when we choose **not** to defend ourselves. After that day my husband never changed what he said— defending me and held to the fact that I was a perfect wife, the best, and that the divorce was his doing alone.

## Working Together for Good

It is an awesome place to be when we watch the Lord at work in our lives. Honestly, I can say that this time I am excited to go *through* it again, because this time I am not just going to make the "best of it"— I am going to enjoy every moment I have alone with the Lord, as my Husband and my children's Father!

The first time I faced divorce, I really didn't know what my future was, so fear made my time alone with Him bittersweet. This time I pressed past the fear and chose to enjoy each day as a special gift from the Lord.

My children and I have fared so wonderfully well because we look for the "good" in everything! And we have seen that *everything* is really better than when I was married, and the children had a father at home. No, this doesn't mean we would have chosen this path, or that the children didn't miss their father. It just means that it's true that God causes all things to work together for good as He promises in Romans 8:28.

My children have all gotten closer to the Lord, to each other, and especially closer to me. My joy has helped them adjust to their new life that had the potential of destroying them—but instead, it has made them better children and young adults.

## Are You Being Called to Ministry?

There are many reasons this has all happened to you and to me. But one thing I believe, I believe that quite possibly God is calling all of us (you, me, my children and RMI) to bigger things, too big for us in our present state. So He has seen fit to bring all of us *through* the refining fire to purify our hearts—it's the same with you, isn't it?

Haven't you noticed the change in your heart, in your life and in your attitude? Divorce or adultery committed against us are the situations that make us and mold us, giving us a new focus on life, a much-needed change in our attitude, and as a result, a brand-new beginning.

One area I needed to be set free from was concern about my reputation—I can happily say, by the grace of God and through much refining, I am finally where I had hoped to be. It has taken many scandals, lies, and rumors, but God was determined that I should never allow people's opinions (good or bad) to affect me or affect the decisions I make.

If you believe the Lord wants to use you in ministry, it will take going *through* some type of refining in order that you never fail to obey God "no matter what" and that you are not going to allow the praise or flattery from people to cause you to fall because they have invested in your pride—which begins by allowing criticism to no longer affect you. If you don't look to the Lord and His opinion, flatter or criticism will always to sway your decision and stop you from doing what God calls you to do.

Don't be shocked or even the least bit surprised when rumors or even lies are spread about you—it is all part of the fires needed to be ready for the Lord's use.

*"Now in a large house there are not only gold and silver vessels, but also vessels of wood and of earthenware, and some to honor and some to dishonor. Therefore, if anyone cleanses himself from these things, he will be a vessel for honor, sanctified, useful to the Master, prepared for every good work" (2 Tim. 2:20–21).*

*"No temptation has overtaken you but such as is common to man; and God is faithful, who will not allow you to be tempted beyond what you are able, but with the temptation will provide the **way** of **escape** also, so that you will be able to endure it" (1 Cor. 10:13).*

*"All **discipline** for the moment seems not to be joyful, but sorrowful; yet to those who have been **trained** by it, afterwards it yields the peaceful fruit of righteousness" (Heb. 12:11).*

We all need to be set free from caring anything at all if we want to travel along our Restoration Journey. This includes lugging the burden of caring about what others think of us, good or bad. If we are going to be used by the Lord and help advance God's kingdom in any big way, we must be willing to carry our cross (whether our cross is in our marriage, our reputation, or in any other crisis God brings into our lives). We must remember that the cross was not only painful—it was also humiliating. It says in Hebrews 12:2 that Jesus "despised the shame" but He still allowed people to mock Him, and He still hung there naked on a cross. Can any of us do less when that is what He did to set us free?

*". . . fixing our eyes on Jesus, the author and perfecter of faith, who for the joy set before Him endured the cross, **despising the shame**, and has sat down at the right hand of the throne of God" (Heb. 12:2).*

## We Need the Right Man in Our Lives

There is no doubt that the Lord longs to be gracious to us, and that He will cause all things to work together for good. Many feel it is *unfair* when *they* have not chosen divorce, since it was their spouse who made the choice. Why do *they* have to both struggle and work toward restoration or at least, why shouldn't they be free to remarry? Having been in both groups, I can say that what men and women are looking for is to be happy and secure, and they believe, as I did, that this means *being* married to someone.

Please understand that I am not a feminist in any sense of the word, however, I can tell you that if we are honest, we have to admit that having a man in our life has never brought the happiness that we dreamed it would and what we have been searching for all of our lives. I am sure this is also true for you men who are reading this: marriage has just never brought about the happiness that we thought it would.

The truth is that just about everyone we know who is currently in a marriage or relationship has been left "wanting." Women, marriage will never fulfill our longing for true love or meet the needs that women have regarding security and being cherished. Only a deep and intimate relationship with the Lord, as our Husband, we being His bride, will meet our deepest needs and longings until our hearts overflow. And once this need in us is met, then we are no longer *vulnerable* to the pitfalls of our neediness, which plagues even young girls in our society today. It is **our** responsibility as older women to break free from this vicious cycle, which is advanced by our attitude and actions when we pursue any **man**.

Men, the needs that you have will never be met by a woman or any other thing you find in the world.

God has shown me there is more peace, joy, and fulfillment that can be yours (and mine), not just when you have a spouse, or when you are restored, but right **now**, because of who God is and who the LORD wants to be to you in your life.

Most of the men and women in our ministry or who read our books are looking for someone to relieve their pain and to find joy in a relationship with someone—when joy and fulfillment is right there within everyone's reach! When my husband left me the first time, I honestly believed that only restoration (when my husband came home) would remove the pain and when I would *finally* be able to be happy again. However, though the pain, due to fear, was relieved once he came home, it was replaced by the same pain and emptiness that most people experience in their marriage.

Truthfully, I felt guilty for feeling this way since God had answered my prayers and had given me the desires of my heart by restoring my marriage. Certainly, I *should* be grateful or at least content once my marriage was restored. But what I found was that I was continually drawn to thinking about the two years when my husband was gone as the happiest of my life (even though they were filled with fear, doubt, and shame)—because of the *intimacy* I had with the Lord and the feeling of love He had for me.

## Intimacy with the Lord is Key

What each woman must do, married or not, is to find her happiness not in herself (as the world or feminist have tried to convince her), not in a man, but in deep intimacy with the Lord that does not come from attending church, but in time spent *alone* with the Lord.

What each man must do, married or not, is to find his happiness not in himself or the things of this world, or in another woman, but in deep intimacy with the Lord that does not come from attending church, but in time spent *alone* with the Lord.

*"Many will say to Me on that day, 'Lord, Lord, did we not prophesy in Your name, and in Your name cast out demons, and in Your name perform many miracles?' And then I will declare to them, **'I never knew you;** depart from Me, you who practice lawlessness'" (Matt. 7:22–23).*

Many times, I have tried to relate these feelings to men and women who are earnestly seeking restoration, but they still believe that if they were to seek the Lord as I have sought Him, it would result in them also being forever single. Not so!

God has a plan for each of our lives, and when we let go of what we want, what we have tried so hard to make happen—then God can take over and give us the abundant life—the life we were created to live. It is living His abundant life where we will find true joy and the fulfillment that every human being is looking for. For me it is to live my life as His bride and to share my life as His bride with women around the world ministering through RMI. For you, the Lord also has a unique and special plan that will thrill your heart and bless you beyond what you could ever have imagined.

*"Things which eye has not seen and ear had not heard, and which have not entered the heart of man, all that God has prepared for those who love Him" (1 Cor. 2:9).*

Finding this intimacy and this abundant life began for me when I started to tell the Lord that **He** is all I needed and wanted as I said in an earlier chapter. When I first began saying this to Him, I only *thought* it in my head, but very soon I *felt* it beginning to fill my heart. Restoration can bring God glory, and certainly the husband/wife relationship is something that is the foundation of our society. However, as a believer, we have to reconcile to the fact that it is our relationship with the Lord that must be paramount in our lives if we are a true believer and not just another religious individual.

The apostle Paul agreed with the principle of the wonderful "opportunity" of remaining single or unmarried when he wrote in First Corinthians 7:32–40:

*"But I want you to **be free from concern** . . . The woman who is unmarried, and the virgin, **is concerned about the things of the Lord**, that she may be holy both in body and spirit; but one who is married is concerned about the things of the world, how she may please her husband.*

*This I say for your own benefit; not to put a restraint upon you, but to promote what is appropriate and to secure undistracted devotion to the Lord.*

*A wife is bound as long as her husband lives; but if her husband is dead, she is free to be married to whom she wishes, only in the Lord. But in my opinion **she is happier if she remains as she is**; and I think that I also have the Spirit of God."*

Nevertheless, what is most important is His plan, His will for our lives. It might be that His plan for you is to have a restored marriage, even for a time, as He had for me. Never fear His plan because only HIS plan will result in the happiness that has evaded you.

This RESTORED marriage testimony will help you understand that once you let go, become His bride, that He may choose to restore you too. So be sure you pray for His will, not what you want or what you are afraid may happen if your husband begins to allure you.

## "God Brought us Full Circle"

As I was sitting in church recently with my husband and children, listening to the preacher, God reminded me that we were in this same place two years prior, but with a broken marriage. God truly has brought everything full circle. As the preacher continued his sermon,

I remembered being at the very same altar two years ago asking the Lord to please give me peace and to show me what I needed to do. I had no idea that everything that would transpire afterward would be for my own good—for I was nowhere near the kind of Godly woman that the Lord needed me to be.

I was not serving the Lord the way I was supposed to be serving Him. I was neither hot nor cold, but lukewarm. I was comfortable going to church and trusting God for things. However, I was not on fire for Him. I did not take pleasure in nurturing the ministry the Lord gave me (my family) through cooking, cleaning, and other household duties. I did not allow my husband to be the leader of our family. I did not listen nor respect him. I was clean on the outside, but filthy on the inside, and I didn't even know it. I was gradually tearing my house down until my life and marriage ended up going down into sinking sand.

While deep in the sand, I humbled myself and prayed to the Lord and repented of my sins. I asked the Lord to make me a better wife to my husband. In my cries to the Lord, He had one of my friends send me the link to *How God Can and Will Restore Your Marriage,* and my eyes began opening wide to the kind of woman I truly was and how I needed to be. I was disobedient to God's Word -- rebellious, contentious, and a Pharisee. Though I asked my husband to forgive me, he already decided that he wanted a divorce and planned to move out of the house as soon as he could. Yet, I knew God would restore my marriage, despite how things appeared, and continued to hold on to His promises. Although I wanted my husband to stop his thoughts and actions of divorce and turn his heart back to me, I began praying and seeking for God's will in my life.

As I trusted God more and more for His will to be done, He provided me with a complete makeover. He took away the victim coat and showed me that I was actually the perpetrator: I was contentious, hateful, bitter, unforgiving, deceitful and loud. I hated being home. The Lord had a lot of work to do within me. It was painful to look in the mirror and see that I wasn't the person I thought I was, not the person others thought I was. Chaste and respectful, one of the lessons I studied while reading *A Wise Woman*, I was not. The Lord was gracious enough to show me that I hadn't embodied any of these Godly qualities, and was a harlot in every sense of the word. The Lord removed all of my ugly, worldly traits layer by layer, and replaced them with fruits of the spirit; love, joy, peace, forbearance, kindness, goodness, faithfulness, gentleness and self-control.

All of the biblical principles discussed in the RMI resources I didn't know to begin with, so I had to re-study them multiple times to sink in. The tests that I underwent after learning and studying of His Word were much harder and painful than the ones from my school days, but they are also more rewarding. I struggled with several things - learning not repaying evil for evil, keeping my mouth shut, and not defending myself. Though difficult, the best part is that the Lord was always with me. He saved me from the fire, and although He may not have always spoken to me in the midst of my testing and trials, He never left me. These tests stretched my faith (especially when I couldn't hear Him) and gave me the endurance that I needed to finish this part of my race.

The most difficult obstacle for me to overcome was fear. The Lord addresses fear many times in His Word. In Isaiah 40:10 NIV, it says "So do not fear, for I am with you; do not be dismayed, for I am your God. I will strengthen you and help you; I will uphold you with my righteous right hand." I clung to my fears - fear of rejection, fear of being hurt again. After the Lord allowed the divorce to go through and He began bringing the wall down between me and my husband and began bringing my husband around, my fear still grew within me and I pushed my former husband away. I pushed him away a few times before the Lord showed me what was happening. He revealed to me that my restoration journey was almost a year longer than it should had because I kept intervening, leaning on my own understanding rather than His. God was putting things back together again, but I was pushing them apart. God was bringing my husband around and allowing my husband to allure me, but I was pushing him away. Once I realized it, I asked the Lord to help me conquer my fear and restore my marriage if it truly was His will.

In His will for my journey, I ended up going through the seasons with the Lord as my Husband twice, due to my fears. The second time around, I learned to relate to every situation and everyone on a different level than before. Each season gave me a deeper appreciation for the Lord as my Husband. While I was going through the seasons with my Love, I was also going through the season with my then former husband. I was and am so in love with the Lord that I had let everything go, but He kept telling me that a life of singleness (as defined by the world) was not His will for me and my children.

The turning point in my journey came about when my former husband continued alluring me, and this time I knew what it was - God's will. We were in *Canaan* Valley, ironically, when the Lord told me that despite my mistakes and fears that He was going to restore my marriage. Wow! There were hints hidden in different things the Lord was showing me. After the Lord's revelation to me, my former husband and I talked even more, but all appeared to stay the same. Then my friend passed away. I was devastated! I watched his marriage get restored not even a month before he died. During this time, my former husband was there to comfort me and my daughter. The Lord used this sorrowful time in my life to bring us even closer together and make our relationship new.

The thought of remarriage to my former husband never crossed my mind. I was happy with the Lord as my Husband and very content living the way that we were. However, the Lord had other plans. My husband decided that he wanted us to get remarried as soon as possible and then the Lord took over from there. This was one of my biggest tests in my journey - overcoming my fears of remarriage and trusting in the Lord. The morning of our wedding ceremony, I was so overcome with fear that when the judge commented about never marrying a bride with cold feet, I nearly passed out. I was praying to the Lord during the entire ceremony to help me conquer my fear and keep obedient to His will; I wanted to run. He reminded me of 1 John 4:18 (NASB) which says that "there is no fear in love, but perfect love casts out fear because fear involves punishment, and the one who fears is not perfected in love." The Lord helped me through the entire ceremony which lasted two minutes but seemed like an eternity.

There has been a whirlwind of changes that the Lord has made in me. Changes that I could not have made on my own. God has been using me to help others in their Restoration Journeys **from the *very beginning* of mine**. I always enjoyed helping others in their time of need, which is why I am a volunteer firefighter, and helping others with their journey, is an extension and a new part of serving others through and for the Lord.  I

also love being home and serving my family now. I am learning so many things about being home, cooking and cleaning. I am still getting brave enough to learn how to quilt, sew, and crochet, as I love to learn. Although I am a work in progress, I am content with being at home and taking care of my first mission field, my family. This is something I always wanted to do but didn't know how until I was led to this ministry.

Now I am starting a new part of this journey with new tests and trials. I am so glad that I had RMI and all of their resources to help me be ready for this part of the journey. I know that this is a lifelong journey and the thing that I want everyone to know is that I love the Lord with all my heart.

I recommend every resource RMI has to offer. They are filled with the truth that every woman coming to this ministry needs. I read all of them at least twice and keep them for future reference. I also suggest writing out the Bible verses that speak to your heart on 3X5 cards. The resources are so wonderful and give you the raw truth while you are broken to help you build a relationship with the Lord as your Husband.

When I found RMI, I was broken and looking for the truth. I found this ministry just when I needed it, which confirms that the Lord's timing is perfect. I couldn't take the RMI courses right away, so I reread what I did have from the ministry, and then moved on to other books like *Workers@Home* about keeping up with my home—another part of His plan.

During this journey, which will last for a lifetime, I found something I never had before, a real relationship with the Lord. When He took me as His bride, my life completely changed. Things that used to matter to me no longer mattered. I wanted and want to live to please Him and do the things He called me to do.

Honestly, I would not change a single minute of the time I spent getting to know my new Husband. It was time that I needed with Him. He is still

my everything and now that I obey Him and have a restored marriage as a result. He has been blessing me so much that I cannot even begin to tell you in just a testimony or praise report. He has given me back everything that I lost over the past two years ago—and so much more. Everything that I allowed the enemy to steal from me since I never tithed and was ignorant to the truth.

I hope that each of you all find Him in a deeper more intimate way, a relationship with Him is worth every tear, heartache, and loss that you will endure.

God's plan is to bring everything full circle as we follow Him along our Restoration Journey.

~ *Casey in West Virginia*

## If I'm not Restored, is Remarrying Someone New an Option?

No matter what your pastor or Christian counselor tells you the Bible does not say *anywhere* that you are free to remarry again. Though God will hold them accountable, you and your children (and grandchildren) will be the ones who will suffer the consequences of your decision to remarry and have to live with a stepparent.

*"Whoever then annuls one of the least of these commandments, and so teaches others, shall be called **least** in the kingdom of heaven; but whoever keeps and teaches them, he shall be called **great** in the kingdom of heaven. For I say to you, that unless your righteousness surpasses that of the scribes and Pharisees, you shall not enter the kingdom of heaven" (Matt. 5:19-20).*

The Bible is clear when you read it that remarriage is not an option but is clearly putting us in the position of being an adulterer or an adulteress.

*"So then if, while her husband is living, she is joined to another man, **she shall be called an adulteress;** but **if her husband dies,** she is free from the law, so that she is not an adulteress, though she is joined to another man" (Rom. 7:3).*

*"A wife is **bound** as long as her husband **lives;** but if her husband is dead, she is free to be married to whom she wishes, only in the Lord.*

*But in my opinion she is happier if she remains as she is; and I think that I also have the Spirit of God" (1 Cor. 7: 39–40).*

My desire to remain unmarried was for many reasons, but ultimately remarriage is not a choice since the Bible (not me, but God says) that remarriage leads to becoming an adulteress. Though society and even people in the church will tell you that remarriage is okay in certain circumstances (yours being one of them), it is **not** the true. Just read the verses. No one needs to interpret what it says. A child can understand it.

*"For the time will come when they will not endure sound doctrine; but wanting to have their ears tickled, they will accumulate for themselves teachers in accordance to their own desires; and will turn away their ears from the Truth, and will turn aside to myths" (2 Tim 4:2-3).*

And as I said earlier, if marriage restoration is His plan for *your* life, then the principle of letting go, especially when it is done "enthusiastically," and pursuing God has proven to be the most powerful principle in the restoration process. The more you put the Lord in first place in our life and in your pursuits, the greater the power and the glory in your life which is magnetic!!

As I said, the more I let go and even went as far to encourage my husband, the more he wanted ME! I was just going the extra mile and it worked in my favor. Soon the woman he was pursuing initially no longer appeared attractive, I did.

And when you have the Lord as your focus, dear reader, it brings about a surrendered heart that results in instant and consistent joy! And because of *my* joy, my husband didn't want to leave as the OW dragged him away, and also my children are also did just as well— grace began flowing like a river in our home and it never stopped!! Though divorce is known to destroy children and families, destruction is not necessary. Once the Lord is truly your Husband, then He, too, will become the Father for your children, which will result in peace and protection that all women long to have for their family.

And as a man, you will find that having God as the head of your home, there will be peace there where there once was turmoil.

## How Will Divorce Affect My Children?

One of the first things I learned is that the way *you feel* about what is happening to you and your family is the key to how well your children will feel. Since this time, I had **joy** (instead of fear, worry, and pain), my children also had **joy**. Since I continued to show respect for their father, they continued showing me (and their father) the same respect.

Honestly, the way my younger children handled the divorce (and even the exposure to the other woman whom he married) has been the biggest revelation. Mothers, **you** alone hold the key to your children's heart. Do you really want to cause it to break? It is in the way *you* act and respond to this difficult situation that will help your children either go through this change effortlessly and almost painlessly, or struggle through it—allowing it to destroy them!

Though my older children (when they were about the same age) were not told about what their father did the first time he left and divorced me (because I did my best to hide everything from them), later, when they grew up, they said that they had no clue what was going on at all, but there was a spirit of fear was in the air, and that is why we all struggled back then to get through it.

Fast-forward to this second time around when I discovered that the principles for *Facing Divorce* can be so powerful, doing it enthusiastically and without fear, that I was determined that my children and I would prosper from what was happening to us, not simply endure it!!

For example, these principles work so well that the first time my husband went to the attorney, I was able to respond to his requests with such agreement and enthusiasm (that are outlined in this book) that he changed his mind within a day, and told me how wonderful I was, apologizing *profusely* for hurting me, and told me that he wanted to work things out and stay! I know you read that once before, but let this sink in! Have you ever heard of this happening with anyone else? And it is not because of me, but because His principles were designed to work this way!

This proves, too, that you cannot *make* your own testimony. If God has a plan for your life that includes a divorce going through, then you cannot stop it by applying these principles, or by praying longer or harder. This time my husband announced the divorce (when I enthusiastically applied the principles, he changed his mind a day later). But RMI had powerful intercessors (in Geneva, Switzerland) that were *crying out to God* to stop my husband from going to the attorney I didn't tell them to pray that way). Their prayers worked, and it was stopped (along with how I responded). However, it didn't take long to realize that the divorce, the scandal, and even the OW were all a part of God's plan for my life.

## Is divorce part of God's plan for your life?

When Jesus was facing the cross, He was able to pray, "Father, not *my* will, but *Your* will be done." How about you? Are you able to trust God enough to go *through* anything in order to be used by Him for a greater glory?

Where would we be if Jesus had refused His cross? Where would we all be had Erin not chosen to go through her husband's adultery and trust God to restore her marriage? Where will you, your children, or other men/women be (the ones *your* live might have helped) if you refuse to take this walk of faith?

God won't force anyone to enter the narrow gate. Though that well-traveled wide road to destruction looks easy, its end is much more pain and ongoing turmoil. Take a look around.

It is my prayer that you instead choose the narrow gate that is not all that hard when we hold His hand— Trust me, I know.

# Chapter 7

# Frightened by Fear

*"Just as Sarah obeyed Abraham, calling him lord,*
*And you have become her children*
*If you do what is right*
*Without being **frightened** by any **fear**."*
—*1 Peter 3:6*

### "Peace in the Midst"

Four weeks ago, I opened the mail finding a letter from my EH's attorney. It told me my EH had filed for divorce and contained copies of some of the legal paperwork one would receive when served. Before RMIEW, that letter would have set me off. I would have collapsed and headed for the phone to call friends and family. I would have hired an attorney. Anger and gossip would have been stirred up all over town.

Instead, I headed for the prayer nest I have made out of some pillows and soft blankets next to my side of the bed. I spoke with my HH. I recited all my memory verses and Psalms. I sang my favorite hymns. I poured out my tears. The Lord kept my children (my two youngest 18 and 22) busy and away most of the weekend. No one knows that a divorce has been filed. This alone is a miracle, as I used to be the biggest talker I knew. Bless the Holy name of Jesus!

My HH is here beside me. I am amazingly calm. I just do the next thing that needs to be done. I am able to focus on blessing others. He is protecting my children, too. Two weeks ago, when I was finally served, it was evening and my daughter was waiting for a friend to arrive. Normally, I wouldn't have answered the door, but I was walking past it. A woman handed me divorce paperwork in a huge envelope!!! If my daughter (who happened to be in the bathroom) had answered the door (she is old enough to have been handed the paperwork in this state), she could not have missed what they were. (My children do not know yet about the divorce filing.) My HH protected her from seeing. I also think the server was very surprised when I smiled and said thank you very pleasantly.

Last week, I was again called to fast, a new thing for me since I joined this ministry in April. The first time I fasted three days, it was very hard. Food has been a comfort thing for me, resulting in me getting fat over the last stressful decade. A year ago though, I began to lose weight, after God helped me make a connection as to why I stress ate. The fasting is a good discipline for me, as it has shown me that I still tend to turn to food when bored or restless, rather than to God. So fasting is helping me get rid of some bad habits, while I focus on the Lord. So, once the fourth of July celebration was over, I began what I thought was a three day fast. However, God called me to extend it, verified that I should extend it again, and I ended up completing a seven day fast! It wasn't easy, but it wasn't awful, and my HH made it clear that I was to continue and when I was to end. No one suspected, and I was able to do all the things listed above during the fast!

I am blessed. God is good. I am cherished, and I am never alone! Praise the Lord!

*~ Beverly in Missouri*

## Signing the Divorce Papers

During my first time through this valley of divorce, I was able, through wisdom and favor, to not *have* to sign my divorce papers. Truthfully, I was so afraid of signing the papers because I learned how God felt about divorce (He hates it), so I was afraid that signing the divorce papers would mean I was an "accomplice" to sin.

It's funny when I think back, because I also knew the principle about submission to our husbands. God tells women to follow only two examples in regard to submission: Jesus (in 1 Peter 2) and Sarah (1 Peter 3). If we look at Sarah's life, we know she was asked by her husband, whom she called lord, to **agree** to be taken as the wife of the Pharaoh, not once, but twice!

Certainly, being an "accomplice" to the degree that Sarah was asked to submit to her husband in no way is any comparison to what God called me to do, which was to sign divorce papers this time. But God is good, He only asks us to do what we are able to do. And at that time in my life, I only had the faith to believe God to deliver me from *having* to sign. I read in Restore Your Marriage that we would favor with our husbands to be released from having to sign, if we exhibited a "gentle and quiet spirit." When I said I would if I needed to, but that he would win by default, that "gentle answer" that turned away all "wrath." I lost by default, but there was no arguing at all.

And God used my earlier testimony to help many other women who read the first *Facing Divorce* book that Erin put together. Many women wrote that they were able to glean from my testimony and the other women who shared their testimonies, and God was faithful to deliver then as well! Here is my 1991 testimony:

In my situation, after read Erin's testimony that led to the beginning of RMI, I also chose to lose my divorce "by default." I took the Scriptures literally when I was served my divorce papers from my husband. I didn't sign the papers, nor did I show up for the hearing— and God delivered me! Like Erin, had I gone to an attorney or shown up in court, I would not have seen the mighty deliverance of the hand of God, because He used my obedience to overturn my divorce a few weeks later!

Our marriage was miraculously restored just three months after the divorce was granted, due in part, because of my obedience to not obtain an attorney. God delivered me when it was discovered that even though the judge had granted the divorce, the papers that had been filed by my husband's attorney were in error. For the divorce "to be legal," his attorney said that my husband would be required to submit additional paperwork to the courts. By the time that this error was discovered—my husband's heart had turned back to me, and he regretted ever filing! When I asked him what he would think if he found out that we were not divorced, he said, "Divorcing you was the biggest mistake of my life!"

My husband was thrilled that God had *somehow* delivered him from being divorced and simply asked (when I told him what his attorney had told me) that I not "tell anyone," which meant not telling the OW. My restoration didn't happen immediately, there were other tests I needed to pass and trials that I had to go through, but God was faithful through it all.

When I first told my husband that I wouldn't contest the divorce and that I wouldn't get an attorney for myself (when I read the RYM book), he was skeptical until he checked that he could get the divorce *without my signing the divorce papers* or showing up in court. In Caroline's case below, her husband **insisted** that she show up. Walking in obedience, while praying to be delivered, as you will see, Caroline helped me go through divorce again, without fear.

## Praising God with Joy Unspeakable!

My eyes are all puffy from crying, not in sadness, but with joy unspeakable! My heart is so very full right now, that it's difficult to really express how wonderful our Lord is, and how grateful I am for this ministry and the blessing that obeying these radical principles has brought me.

God used my obedience in not getting an attorney, not listening to my mom, dad, or even my pastor, all of whom strongly tried to inform me that I didn't have to just "roll over" in these proceedings. They wanted me to get an aggressive attorney who would really make my husband feel dire consequences for his current conduct.

By God's awesome and incredible grace, and through I'm sure, the prayers of my ePartner and the RYM members; today I obeyed these principles and trusted God.

Not only did God bring financial blessing in the hearing (that I was firmly asked to attend by my husband today), God also used me as a witness to the court representative, who never saw "such agreeable and nice people" in all her years of participation in some of the 19,000 divorces in our county. (God help us!)

But most important to me, after over six months of separation and years of my contentious behavior, I finally saw my husband's wall of hate come down before my very eyes!! As we talked about money and custody issues over the course of these two hours, God shut my mouth and only opened it when I had something **fabulous to say about my husband**: his integrity, his great earning capacity, his care of the children, and his responsible way of providing all of our needs and managing our money! Although I repented early on in this "spiritual adventure," my husband was not open to hear anything I wanted to confess (I'm sure, because he had heard "religious" things out of my arrogant, self-righteous mouth many times before). God continued changing me, so I just waited.

Today, God gave me the chance to admit to my husband (and to the clerk): my problems in handling money, my disorganization, my irresponsibility, and the past problems I have had in using strong pharmaceuticals (legitimately, but now, praise God, I'm off them!) to manage my chronic pain.

By the end of the "interview," when I admitted to being "flaky," my husband actually contradicted me, and praised me in front of the clerk. He said that I could really produce great things when I put my mind to it!! He also said that I was sensitive and caring with the children, and how very understanding I am about his demanding work schedule! Talk about BLOTTING OUT the memory! I nagged him CONSTANTLY about his work for the last 10 years! And I didn't even ask God for that one! Praise Him! He knew I needed it!

Whereas before when we saw each other he was aloof and abrupt, never looking at me or talking more than he absolutely had to; today he took the elevator down with me (I'm disabled) instead of the stairs. Then he walked out of the building with me, shared with me something of what his day was going to be like, and then (Hallelujah!), he agreed to have dinner with us tomorrow night! I heard myself say, "If it gets too hard to get away from work, don't get stressed about it. I won't tell the kids; in case you can't make it." (Huh!? I know where THAT came from and it wasn't me!)

He said, with conviction, "I will make it happen!" Then he called out, "See you tomorrow," as he ran to his car. If you had any inkling of what his work is like, you'd be hopping up and down in praise that our God could turn his heart enough to even SAY something like that!

I come to the site to read praise reports when I am feeling discouraged. Just raising my voice in praise to God for what He's doing for others lifts my countenance and causes "mountain moving faith" to rise up in me. So please, please dear sister, take time right now to use your voice in thanksgiving and praise to our magnificent, living Lord, who can take even a court hearing and use it to His good! And "take courage" that God is working on your behalf, even as you obey Him right this minute!

~ *Caroline in Kentucky*

How many of you have ever heard of a report like that regarding a divorce hearing? Never. Instead, everyone loves to share divorce "horror stories" to scare you into getting a "good" lawyer. Just remember, "A thousand may fall at your side, and ten thousand at your right hand, but **it shall not approach you**" (Ps. 91:7). Instead, "Do not be overcome by evil, but overcome evil with good" (Rom. 12:21). Release your attorney and trust God **alone** to deliver and protect you. Pray for opportunities to *bless* your husband before and even during the divorce, if you are unable to forgo showing up for the hearing.

If your husband asks you to sign, no matter what the divorce papers say, you are not an accomplice to a crime, you are instead following the principles that Jesus told us to do that will bring victory. First, He said that we should not resist any evil (that includes divorce), that we should not only *agree* to walk that mile, but then go the second mile (and without being asked), and that when we are sued (this means being sued for divorce) then we should give whatever is asked, then go beyond and give more!

This is not my crazy idea, but God's. How Christian counselors, pastors, and Christian friends can ignore this principle, I have no idea. Here is the verse again. Read it to see how clear God is about what we are supposed to do versus what everyone else is telling you to do.

*"You have heard that it was said, 'an eye for an eye, and a tooth for a tooth.' But I say to you, do not resist an evil person; but whoever slaps you on your right cheek, turn the other to him also. If anyone wants to sue you and take your shirt, let him have your coat also. Whoever forces you to go one mile, go with him two. Give to him who asks of you, and do not turn away from him who wants to borrow from you" (Matt. 5:38–42).*

Caroline had the victory and the joy that now makes her weep, because she went to court (because her husband insisted) humbly and trusted God. She knew and applied the principles that not only got her *through* the hearing peacefully, but also brought the wall of hate down as she blessed her husband in the most radical of occasions!

Here are some more versus that few pastors or Christians know or encourage you to follow.

*"Does any one of you, when he has a case against his neighbor, dare to go to law before the unrighteous, and not before the saints?" (1 Cor. 6:1).*

This is a very firm Scripture. Would we dare God? If you merely choose to show up in court, you are standing "before the unrighteous." Some believe that this is their opportunity to *fix* their situation—not so. Caroline did not *choose* to show up; her husband pressed it upon her. She prayed to be delivered, but God had other plans.

*"For My thoughts are not your thoughts, nor are your ways My ways,' declares the LORD. For as the heavens are higher than the earth, so are My ways higher than your ways and My thoughts than your thoughts" (Is. 55:8–9).*

When we lean unto our own understanding and make our own plan, God will simply step aside and allow you to fall so that you learn that His plan is far and above your plan. Once again, walk in obedience and if you need to, pray to be delivered, but just remember, you are blessed if you must go *through* the fiery furnace of a hearing—God has a bigger plan and will bless you because you went *through* trusting in Him. However, do not **choose** to jump into the fiery furnace, or you might just find yourself a martyr without a cause!

Yet as difficult as not retaining an attorney and refusing to fight for financial support is, there are some who are being called higher, like Janet in Pennsylvania:

## Jesus, Our Source!

I praise the Lord for His strength that is perfect in our weaknesses. He put it on my heart for several months to drop the spousal support I receive from my husband. I knew to do it but was fearful about making it with our two girls.

One night, God spoke to me again on the subject. I told my husband I was willing to drop the spousal and child support. He was shocked. He immediately asked me how I would make it. I replied I would make it.

He appreciated my dropping the spousal support but would not allow me to drop the child support. He would not feel right if he were not supporting our girls. He was grateful, and I was obedient.

When I hung up, an **immediate peace overtook my heart and mind**. I began praying and receiving a breakthrough in my intercession like I had not in a long time. I would make it by the grace of God. Jesus is our source—be blessed and be obedient. Trust and obey—there is no other way.

~ *Janet in Pennsylvania*


Peace, and an open door to God, is something we cannot put a price tag on. And when we are willing, like Janet, to step out in faith, God will bless us.

## We shall Judge Angels?

*"Or do you not know that the saints will judge the world? And if the world is judged by you, are you not competent to constitute the smallest law courts? Do you not know that **we shall judge angels?** How much more, matters of this life?" (1 Cor. 6:2–3).*

In this verse God is mocking us, showing us how petty and insignificant the matters of this world are in comparison to our life is *with* Him.

If we are fearful of how the courts will treat us and try to appeal to them (or our husbands or wives), we will miss God's blessings. God is able to turn the heart of kings, judges, attorneys and wives/husbands: their hearts are in God's hand too.

*"The king's **heart** is like channels of water in the hand of the LORD; He **turns** it wherever He wishes" (Prov. 21:1).*

And it is when God sees **our** heart: someone who trusts Him, someone who joyfully follows His principles, and believes His promises—this is what causes Him to turn that other heart towards us!

*"If then you have law courts **dealing with matters of this life,** do you appoint them as judges who are of no account in the church?" (1 Cor. 6:4).*

The courts in my country (the United States of America) no longer follow biblical teachings as they did when this country was founded. As a result, we have rulings and burdens placed upon believers that neither God nor our founding fathers had in mind. If you choose the courts to help you, you will choose their judgment over God's protection and provisions.

*Proverbs 29:26 says clearly, "Many seek the ruler's favor, but justice for man comes from the LORD."*

Even in countries that allow you a few years to have to wait for a divorce, if you simply say that you don't want it, will result in your husband/wife loathing you because you are standing in the way of what he/she believes will make him/her happy?!? You would do better to get out of the way of the wicked (Psalm 1:1), stop resisting evil and go the other mile, give your coat (Matthew 5:39), and watch God show up.

This is also true for feeling that you have to make a statement that you don't *want* a divorce.

I really believed the first time I faced divorce that I had to make it clear to my husband that divorce was nothing I *wanted*, once again, because I feared I would not be an accomplice to the crime of divorce and end up like **Ananias'** Sapphira! (See Acts 5.) But this time I was well aware that God **knew** my heart, and He *knows* your heart too. He knew I didn't *want* a divorce, and that for me to make sure I stated it to my husband would mean I was still a Pharisee of the worst kind.

However, if you are the one who kept speaking or threatening divorce, or you were the one who initiated it, then stating that you don't want one would certainly be warranted and a very good idea. Don't keep stating it, just make it clear it was a mistake if you were the one who spoke of it.

In Kris' situation, you will read that God called her, too, to a higher level of faith and obedience. It was her testimony and faith, along with Vivian's (that you will read immediately after Kris') that gave ME the faith and courage to sign the divorce papers this time when my husband asked me to!!

## I am Truly a New Creature in Christ!!

"I wanted to take a moment to praise my Lord and Saviour. He will give you the grace and peace to walk through anything if you only open your heart up to Him.

My husband came by Friday and asked me to *sign* the final divorce decree. I was able to do this with a smile and without the "scene" that would have happened just five months ago. I am so thankful to the Lord for giving me the blessed opportunity to show HIM that I have changed. The Lord gave me the chance to see what His love, and faith in Him, has done to change me. The Lord has shown me I am truly a new creature in Christ, and I could not be more thankful.

I have been so blessed as the Lord delayed the court proceedings and caused confusion at every turn, but now, this is truly in the Lord's hands. From my understanding at this point, my husband and his attorney can just go to the court house any day, ask to be added to the docket, and the judge will sign the decree. I am not needed and will not receive any more notifications before it becomes final.

Either the Lord will deliver me and part the Red Sea, or I will go through this test. Either way, I am unafraid and steadfast. I would be lying if I said there were not a few tears after my husband left, but the words "I quit" did not ever enter my head. The Lord promised me that He would be with me; He promised His Word was good; He promised deliverance; He promised restoration, if I was steadfast; He did not promise that this would not be uncomfortable or even hurt. So, this is another step that hurts a little, it is not the end. The Lord can stop this divorce, but even if it needs to go through for His perfect plan, then I will wait to see this thing the Lord is going to do for me.

So, I thank and praise my Lord and heavenly Father for all He has done, and is doing in not only my marriage, but in me! I thank Him that no matter what I see, He is working and taking care of my husband and my children. I thank Him that I was able to faint not and show my husband the joy and peace that comes from the Lord!

If you seem to be approaching, or are at the place I am right now, DO NOT GIVE UP! Trust in the Lord and stay on the path. Weeping may last for a night, but joy really will come in the morning. God Bless!"

*~ Kris in Texas*

**A month later RMI received this email from Kris:**

Dear Erin and all the wonderful people at RMI,

I just wanted to thank you for putting my praise report about signing the divorce papers in the April newsletter. It was a timely reminder of all that the Lord has done in my life, as the divorce did indeed go through in March. Some women have asked me whether or not I would do everything like I did (letting my attorney go, signing as I was asked to, etc.), knowing that the Lord would still have let the divorce go through. The answer is a simple yes. I would do it the same way again.

I could be bitter (as I have seen many others do) and lament that because I did all the Lord showed Erin to do and He still did not stop the divorce in my case that I did it all wrong, and I guess that anger could spill over to all areas in my life, including in my walk with God. BUT just because it may not have had the "desired outcome" as some see it, I still did what the Lord directed me to do, so it did have the exact outcome the Lord had in mind, which in turn is the desired outcome for me also. I would give other women the same advise as in the *Facing Divorce* book without hesitation or reservation, because I believe the advise is straight from the Lord.

Of all the things that have run through my mind (and that I have battled with theses last couple of weeks), that I should have done things connected with the divorce differently following RYM principles is not one of them. I believe I will see the goodness of the Lord in the land of the living, and that all things truly work for His good, and that someday He will have a testimony in me to prove that very thing!

May the Lord richly bless you all at RMI!

*~ Kris in Texas*

## Husband's Attorney Prays for No Divorce!

I went to my husband's lawyer during my lunch break two days ago to sign the consent forms. I asked God to go before me and to be my rear guard. Praise God, He was so faithful!

When I went to sign the papers in obedience to my husband, his lawyer asked me if I was sure I wanted to go through with this. I looked at her and said I was okay with it. She asked if I was going to the hearing a week later. I said no, since it was not compulsory for me to do so.

She asked me, "Wouldn't you like to see your husband." I don't think I answered. But with her questioning, my eyes were beginning to tear. I hope she hadn't noticed. She asked me if I had thought of asking my husband out. I said no. She said we both seemed so nice, we were able to settle everything by e-mail. I said that my husband is a very nice man.

She said, "Why don't you two try again?" I said I was a terrible wife. She asked why we didn't meet? I said I would leave it to my husband. She smiled and said that she would speak to him to ask me out! She said that with the hearing, the decree nisi (temporary divorce) would be approved. And after three months, it would be absolute. She was so nice—I really felt like I was going to breakdown and cry

Then she asked me if I still went to church. I said yes. She said that my husband told her that he went to church too! She smiled again and said that she would pray for us. She told me not to lose hope. She encouraged me and said there was still three months before the divorce becomes absolute. All the while, I was trying not to cry. As I walked out, she told me that there are problems in every new marriage and not to worry.

I never thought I would walk out of a lawyer's office after signing papers consenting to a divorce, feeling encouraged! Even my husband's lawyer is praying for us! Look at how God works!

Indeed, a man's mind plans his ways, but the Lord directs His steps! I am still praying that God will stop the divorce if it be His will, but if He does allow it to go through, I pray that He will use it for GOOD!

Wow Lord, You are so awesome!

~ *Vivian in Singapore*

## Why I Had to Sign

When my husband approached me about the divorce—again, he told me that he was going to have me take on ALL of our family and business debt, and that he was not going to pay child support, again.

And let me interject something I think you each should know and understand. Because my husband knew about my part in RMI for years, which led to us being restored, he knew every conviction I had. And so he used my convictions against me. He took full and complete advantage of me. Did you hear what I said? He took advantage of my convictions and abused the principles I believed, and he knew I would follow! That is why he knew he could "get away with" not paying child support, leaving behind all of the debt, etc., etc.

It's important that you understand what I just said because so many of you are *afraid* that if you do what is right that you will be taken advantage of. So God in His wisdom and love for **you** sent me and many others ahead and "set us up" by making sure He put us in very difficult predicaments and allowed us each to walk through different and very difficult valleys for your sake.

This time I was not naïve or ignorant of what was going on as I was the first time. This time I knew fully what he was planning to do and due to feeling His love for me, I willingly laid down my life.

"For this reason the Father loves Me, because I lay down My life so that I may take it again. No one has taken it away from Me, but I lay it down on My own initiative" (John 10:16-18).

This is why I "enthusiastically" agreed, because my husband knew that I did not *want* to sign the divorce papers, but when he explained this to his attorney, he was told that the judge would **never** agree to "no child support" unless I signed the papers. And remember this dear reader, if you are asked to sign it will not make it any more difficult for God to restore your marriage!

*"Behold, I am the LORD, the God of all flesh; is anything too difficult for Me?" (Jeremiah 32:27).* Will you answer by saying...

*"Ah Lord GOD! Behold, You have made the heavens and the earth by Your great power and by Your outstretched arm! Nothing is too difficult for You"! (Jeremiah 32:17)* ...as is chose to do?

Knowing that God was calling me to a higher level of obedience and trust in Him, I "enthusiastically" told my husband I would sign when he told me what his attorney had said! I had no idea when I would be asked to sign, but would you believe that God led me to Second Chronicles 20:6–25 the day BEFORE I was asked to sign the final divorce papers! As I said, I did not know that I would be asked to sign the papers the next day, but God did! I read,

*"When the enemy was coming against Jehoshaphat, he cried out to the Lord, "O LORD, the God of our fathers, are You not God in the heavens? And are You not ruler over all the kingdoms of the nations? Power and might are in Your hand so that no one can stand against You."*

*"Should evil come upon us, the sword, or judgment, or pestilence, or famine, we will stand before this house and before You (for Your name is in this house) and cry to You in our distress, and You will hear and deliver us . . . How they are rewarding us by coming to*

*drive us out from Your possession which You have given us as an inheritance."*

*"O our God, will You not judge them? For we are powerless before this great multitude who are coming against us; nor do we know what to do, **but our eyes are on You.**"*

*". . . Thus says the LORD to you, 'Do not fear or be dismayed because of this great multitude, for **the battle is not yours but God's.**'"*

*"**Tomorrow** go down against them . . . You need not fight in this battle; station yourselves, stand and see the salvation of the LORD on your behalf . . . Do not fear or be dismayed; **tomorrow** go out to face them, for the LORD is with you.'"*

This is where the Lord took me the day **before** I was asked to sign the final divorce papers! It wasn't until that evening that I again went to this passage and noticed that it says *twice* that I needed to go out **tomorrow!** That was more of a confirmation than I needed—but maybe this is what **you** needed to hear to help you when you are asked!!

As a result of the Word from the Lord for Jehoshaphat, he responded to the Lord by bowing *"his head with his face to the ground,* and . . . fell down before the LORD, **worshiping the LORD.**" And then "stood up to praise the LORD God of Israel, with a **very loud voice.**"

**What were the results of this trust and praise to the Lord?**

**His enemies destroyed themselves!!!!**

It says, "They rose early in the morning and went out . . . and when they went out, Jehoshaphat stood and said, 'Listen to me, O Judah and inhabitants of Jerusalem, **put your trust in the LORD your**

**God and you will be established**. Put your trust in His prophets and succeed.'"

*"Give thanks to the LORD, for His lovingkindness is everlasting."*

**They gave thanks before God did anything!!**

"When they began **singing** and **praising,** the LORD *set ambushes . . . destroying them completely*; and when they had finished . . . they *helped to destroy one another"!!*—"no one had escaped."

And if that were not enough . . .

"When Jehoshaphat and his people came to take their spoil, they found much among them, including goods, garments, and valuable things which they took for themselves, more than they could carry. And they were **three days** taking the spoil because there was so much"!!

The day I was asked to sign the divorce papers was a day **full** of appointments. I knew this had to be part of God's plan, so that I would be too busy to let my mind dwell on what I was about to do, which may have caused me to fear or have anxiety. When I walked in to sign, I had absolutely no fear. I was able to be excited, and enthusiastic with the paralegal who led me to the room to sign them. My hands did not shake or tremble. Ladies, this was God!! He had prepared me for this "day of battle" and I knew He was going to fight for me.

Had it not been for Kris' and Vivian's testimony, I know I would not have been able to sign the papers "fear free"! God tells us that we will be able to overcome the wicked one (who, by the way, is not your husband/wife or the OW/OM) by the blood of the Lamb and the **word of *their* testimony**. (Read Revelation 12:11.)

Always keep in mind that what God is asking you to go *through* today or tomorrow will someday be the one testimony that enables someone else to be able to go *through* something else also "fear free"! I am grateful for Kris and Vivian who built the bridge to "sign fear free" for you and me!

# Chapter 8

# Frightened by Fear
# Part 2

*"If you do **what is right**
Without being frightened by any fear."*
—1 Peter 3:6

There are many ways that fear will try to overtake you. One that is running rampant is the fear of our spouse being unfaithful—committing adultery.

Though you may have already faced, and hopefully, conquered this fear, it would do you well to read the chapter about adultery in Erin's book, *How God Can and Will Restore Your Marriage*, which gave me the foundational principles regarding unfaithfulness and how to overcome the devastating effects of adultery through the use of Scripture. And since this sin is so prevalent in our society and within the church, I felt the Lord leading me to devote one chapter to discuss when unfaithfulness is "suspected" but not yet confirmed. I hope this will help other men/women who may be facing the *possibility* that their wife/husband has been with another man/woman or as we refer to them in RMI as the OW "other woman" or OM "other man."

This time around, I had absolutely no idea adultery was happening again; the first time I had my suspicions. But this time, believe it or not, it was our *counseling* pastor who kept telling me, "He has to be involved with another woman; he has all the signs!"

Let me stop and share that I am **more** against counseling and counselors than ever before—even more than Erin is. It was our senior pastor who told me (and my husband) that unless we went to counseling, we would be removed from our church. I did go, but not surprisingly, my ex-husband never would go.

There are so many reasons I am personally against counseling— this is just one issue that brought out the holy anger in me against counselors and counseling—when I experienced firsthand how often they plant the thoughts in the minds of a hurting wife or broken husband that their spouse is *probably* committing adultery!!

All I could think about was how a spiritually unstable most women and men are in the church! Many women would be so devastated; they could easily run out and commit adultery themselves, or worse, take their own lives (and even her children's lives like a wife did in California)!

The other thing that usually happens when this seed is planted —they *foolishly* **confront** their husbands/wives and ask them flat out if they are seeing someone or are having an affair!

Dear reader, there is no greater mistake (other than committing adultery to pay your spouse back) than to ask them to 'fess up' or confront them! If you suspect your spouse is involved with someone else, then get on your face before God and get ready for the battle— spiritually! Get prayed up, get close with the Lord; let Him guide you, comfort you, and get you ready for what *may* be up ahead.

And also, **do not give the *enemy* the advantage He has given you** by confronting and letting the sin of adultery out of its closet! It is much better that they (your husband/wife and the person they are involved with) to continue to be forced to **sneak around** than it will be when it is out in the open and they flaunt it in front of your face! This is exactly what happens when you confront someone who is cheating and try to get your spouse to confess. And not only is it flaunted in front of your face, but that's when they'll also tell your children (introducing them and their visits are with them) and they begin to run around together in your community!

Adultery, ladies and gentlemen, is a **spiritual** battle; therefore, you need to use *wisdom* (not acting on your emotions) when fighting it.

*"If the axe is dull and he does not sharpen its edge, then he must exert more strength. Wisdom has the advantage of giving success"* (Eccl. 10:10).

In war you certainly would not let the enemy know that you are aware of their moves, would you? Instead, you would conceal this knowledge to be ready for the next time the enemy attacks! And when you *give* them the advantage, by telling them that you know or suspect what they're up to, then they will use this *against* you! I experienced this the first time my husband cheated on me and have seen it countless times with women I help minister to.

From the moment adultery is confronted, the OW or OM has the advantage in your spouse's life! This is the honest to God's truth! No longer will your spouse be sneaking around so you don't find out, but instead their sin will be flaunted in front of your face and soon your spouse will bombard your ears with junk, I promise, you do *not* want to hear!

The first time I was facing divorce, I heard of no one else who had ever attempted it. It was before I knew about RMI. So, when the enemy set me up to discover that my husband was not living alone in a dumpy apartment (which is why he said he didn't want me or the children to know where he lived), but was living with another woman in the best part of town, I took the bait of the enemy and told my husband I knew.

That night he cried, confessed it was true, and that night was also the very last time he stayed until the children went to bed (so I would not be suspicious he was living with someone else). Instead, after the night I confronted him, he would tell me that he had to get "home to her" poor thing, who was alone, etc., etc.

The same thing will happen to you! Don't fall for this trap if you haven't taken the bait already.

Fast forward to this time. This time I did not suspect there was anyone, but as I said when I was forced to go to counseling (or be asked to leave my church), it was the counseling pastor who told me that there was no doubt my husband was involved with someone. That very same day my younger sister told me I was so stupid, of course he was involved with someone again since this was the kind of man he was. Each time I dismissed it. But that evening it began to eat just slightly in my gut.

So, as I always was faithful to do, and what you need to train yourself to do too, is that I snuck away to get alone with the Lord until that feeling was gone. And as I always was faithful to do, I told Him what had been said to me (not for His benefit, He always knows, but it helps to tell Him), and then I surprised myself by asking if it were true (when I *knew* it wasn't); do you understand what I mean? It was like the Lord had prompted me to ask what I really believed was not true. But He startled me and said, "Yes, it IS true."

BUT because HE told me, and I had not stupidly gone to find out for myself, or snoop or confront my husband with my suspicions like I did before or what many of you are doing, it did not hurt, nor was I shaken!!

Psalm 55:22 says, "Cast your burden upon the LORD and He will sustain you; He will never allow the righteous to be shaken."

This time I was determined not to make the same mistake, as before, so I did not mention anything to my husband about it. God had even told me her name while I was alone with Him in my prayer closet. And He also revealed to me each of the times they were together, when it was right under my nose, but never suspected a thing!

Two things I want you to know, first, when the Lord was all done revealing the truth to me, He asked me how I felt. I had to sort of examine myself, just like when your physician asks you where the pain is, or if you feel pain. When I did, I realized there was **no pain at all**—no fear—there was nothing but wonderful peace! This was certainly a far cry (literal cry) from the first time I found out about the first OW.

*And please don't be cruel enough to think that since it happened before I was "used" to it! No one can get used to betrayal no matter how many times it happens. You can harden yourself to it, but hardheartedness is no remedy.

Secondly, I asked the Lord *why* I had not even noticed these things that were so obvious. Was I stupid; was I naïve, etc. like the two people (the counseling pastor and my sister) who said he was involved had said to me?

The Lord told me something that I believe will help you too. He told me that it was because each of us looks at other people they way we are! Meaning, someone who is a liar always thinks other people are lying to them, right? So, it was my pure heart that looked at my husband with the same pure heart as I had. That I would never be unfaithful to him, so surely, he wouldn't be unfaithful to me either.

That's why doing foolish things, like snooping is so dangerous. Snooping is another way a man or woman responds when the seed is planted that their spouse is "having an affair," which I prefer to state as "committing adultery." Sin, in my opinion and in Erin's opinion and in God's opinion, is *not* a **party** or "affair." Adultery is sin and needs to be addressed the way that it is sin by calling it adultery.

That's why it's so dangerous when you begin to snoop— it will uncover the **pain** that God had tried to protect you from. Some women will not be able to overcome that pain, and often, after uncovering more evidence of her husband's sin, will fall into the other traps already discussed: committing adultery herself or confronting her husband with what she found in her snoop! Some women, as I said, are so overwhelmed that the do the unthinkable like killing their husbands or taking their own lives. We hear it all the time on the news, right?

Men who snoop often respond to their pain and betrayal with anger, and sometimes violence! There is no other way to destroy your future or make that other man appear the one your wife wants, than by getting into a fight with the other man she is involved with. Unfortunately, the anger is often directed at your wife who you either verbal assault or physically hurt, and that will be added to the negative feelings she has for you already. Don't confront!

# Chapter 9

# Spying and Following

*"There is no fear in love...*
*and the one who fears is not perfected in love"*
—1 John 4:18

Someone who suspects their spouse is cheating on them prefers a higher level of snooping by spying or following their spouse. Wow, what a bad and fatal decision this is! Some of the saddest stories I hear are when mothers or fathers take their own children with them when following their spouse to the apartment of the OW or OM. And if that were not enough, some even take the children to the door to confront their spouse—seeing their own father or mother caught in the act of being with this other person and the fight that goes with will be something children will never forget! Talk about damaging your children for life; what a vivid picture that they will be haunted with!! And this is because you can't help but act like a madman or hysterical woman—this is PAIN. Think of an animal being shot...it runs around mad, out of control.

Once I was the first person who came upon a horrible car accident. The one boy was running around out of his mind seeing his cousin who he was sure was dead or dying. Later we found out that this boy who was running had two broken legs! I also, to my horror, saw a boy from our high school hit by a car and thrown in the air, then get up and run away. Later we found out his leg had been broken in five places and his hip was shattered yet out of shock he could still run!

Emotional pain will do this same thing. So, like I did with that young boy, I want to encourage you to **sit down**, *remain calm*, because I assure you that everything will be all right. You will get *through* this, but don't cause any more damage than what has already been done.

Also, all of these responses are exactly what the world would do and even tell you to do! As I said, I fell into this trap and you may already have taken the bait too. But if you haven't or your friend hasn't, then make sure they listen to what will happen if they foolishly confront their husband or wife with what they know or suspect.

Once again, let me tell you that the first time my husband was unfaithful (during my first restoration), I made the mistake of telling my husband that I knew he was living with another woman. I knew he was living with someone because the enemy left "bait" (which he always does) of something that seemed "odd" that made me suspect there was someone.

When I told my husband that I knew, he cried, said he was sorry, but lived with her for another year! But it did *not* stop what he was doing, I had basically given the OW my husband on a silver platter—and she took full advantage of it.

From that moment on, my husband had to tell **me** that he couldn't stay, that he had to hurry *home* to **her**! Only a day earlier, he would stick around so I wouldn't *suspect* that he was living with someone. Oh, what one foolish decision can do!

So is there a godly way when discovering that your husband has been unfaithful in his marriage to you? Yes. Let me share this again with more details.

This time, years later, I was much more prepared. I was told *by our counseling pastor* many times during our counseling session (oh, God help us!) that there was no doubt that my husband was "once again" involved with another woman, but I kept telling him that he was wrong. On the very same day my sister told me the same thing, "Hey, he has a pattern with adultery, don't be so stupid." But again, I said that she was mistaken.

Later that day, however, I could hear those words (from my sister and the counseling pastor) echoing in my ears, which caused my spirit (in my gut) to begin to experience **fear**. But rather than ignore or give into my fear, I *immediately* got up and went into my prayer closet, to be alone with the Lord, so I could find my peace again. I went there to feel better, but then the Holy Spirit prompted me to ask if adultery was true.

As soon as I asked (which my mind was saying "why ask when you know it's not true?") ever so lovingly and gently, the Lord revealed to me that it was true by showing me in my mind each and every encounter that he had had with her. He even told me her name and showed me the picture of when we had all met at my husband's reunion two years earlier! The Lord laid out all the evidence before my mind in a matter of seconds. But the revelation and truth came without *any* pain or fear, because it came from the One who give us His "perfect love" that casts out all fear!

*"There is no fear in love; but perfect love casts out fear, because fear involves punishment, and the one who fears is not perfected in love" (1 John 4:18).*

Let me again remind you, so that if you have questions you need to ask the Lord. I asked Him why I hadn't realized what was going on? That's when He told me that it was because I had faith like a child, and that I had had my eyes on Him. He did not scold me for being "stupid or naïve." Instead, He protected me from experiencing any pain and waited to show me Himself, when I needed to know what was going on. And because I had been keeping my eyes on Him only, when I was told—He is the One who told me—so that He could also bring with the news perfect peace to accompany the normally devastating truth.

Later that evening, and some of the days that followed, the thought of what I knew (that there was another woman and adultery again) would try to overwhelm me with fear and rattle my heart. But at the very first sign of it, I would get alone with the Lord and seek Him for my peace again. Usually He would prompt me to tell Him how I felt about Him, to which I would respond, "Lord, You are all I want, You are all I need, You are the only One I live for!" This encounter would replace my fear with abundant joy! **I would leave my prayer closet rejuvenated knowing that I had a Lover too who was not sinful but what was what I was designed to be—His bride!**

It was almost three weeks later that my husband announced that he was seeing "someone." The announcement came without warning, but God had prepared me since I already knew he was "seeing" someone since He had told me three weeks earlier. My husband did not confess that he had been involved with her *before* he filed for divorce, but I didn't need to hear that from him, because the Lord already told me the whole truth.

It was because God had prepared me that I did not shake or even tremble! Instead, when he confessed he was seeing "someone" I told him how nice it was for him to have found someone so quickly, that I was sure that they would be happy, and without thinking even said her name a couple of times even though my husband had never once mentioned her name to me! Praise God he didn't drive off the road when it popped out of my mouth—he was clearly shaken— while I sat there feeling so loved and cherished by the Lord.

Not only was my husband in shock when I said the OW's name, because I kept saying her name over and over again. Without knowing it, saying her name without tears actually hurt my husband since it proved to him that I really didn't care—God had turned the tables! Usually we who are cheated on sit there hurt, devastated, while our spouse sits there telling us how much they love someone else and not us! But when you do things God's way, He has a different plan.

My husband was so hurt because during my first go 'round with his adultery, it left me so fearful that he knew I could never even *say* the OW's name, and even hearing her name said by anyone else made me feel like I would throw up—for years! Since he had seen me working in ministry for nearly five years before he left again, my husband knew this entire story that I shared with many women when I ministered to them. So by my saying her name, which I had not planned to do, the pain left my heart and went into his.

This time, God had given me a huge advantage, so instead of being on the defensive, I was able to take the offensive: Offense, however, does **not** mean being offensive or on the attack. It simply means that we are not taking the defensive position: cowered in a corner, terrified, or running wild in pain doing foolish things.

So whether you are suspicious that there may be someone else, or especially if you have a friend, co-worker, mother, father, brother or sister going through this who is suspicious (or people are telling you things), please tell them my testimony and the wisdom so that they can "fight the good fight (spiritually) and finish the course" (2 Tim. 4:7)!

God knows everything—right? And He will faithfully tell you, ever so gently, what is going on just at the right time, and He will do it *lovingly* so you will not be hurt from it! Whenever we do things according to His will, we will reap blessings in the midst of all of the trials that destroy most people—especially Christians!

*"Instead of your shame you will have a **double** portion, and instead of humiliation they will shout for joy over their portion. Therefore they will possess a **double** portion in their land, Everlasting joy will be theirs" (Isa. 61:7).*

So many Christians are ignorant of His ways. They look at things and react in the exact same way as the people who are not believers. When evil gets more intense, and it seems like their spouse or ex-spouse is prospering while they are getting hit with all kinds of stuff from every which way, they begin to doubt God's ability to help them and turn back to doing things for themselves. How foolish!

Here is a principle that all Christians should know and keep close to their heart throughout their lives and something they need to teach to their children:

Whenever you see wickedness increasing it only means that the evil is getting closer to being destroyed FOREVER.

*"A senseless man has no knowledge, nor does a stupid man understand this: That when the wicked sprouted up like grass and all who did iniquity flourished, it was only that they might be destroyed forevermore" (Ps. 92:6–7).*

Yes, that sin destroyed forever!!

May this promise stay close to your heart, guide your steps and govern your actions.

# Chapter 10

# Backed to the Red Sea Financially

*"Whoever slaps you on your right cheek,*
*Turn the other to him also."*
*—Matthew 5:39*

When faced with divorce papers, which has become, for the most part, *nothing* about saving the marriage, but instead has become a financial and possession tug-of-war, most Christians try to give only what they believe is "fair," or what they believe their spouse deserves—but this is unbiblical. It is **not** the way God treats us, nor is it the example Jesus gave us when He lived amongst mankind nor what taught us when He ministered here on earth. He said…

*"You have heard that it was said, 'an eye for an eye, and a tooth for a tooth.' But I say to you, do not resist an evil person; but whoever slaps you on your right cheek, turn the other to him also. If anyone wants to sue you and take your shirt, let him have your coat also. Whoever forces you to go one mile, go with him two. Give to him who asks of you, and do not turn away from him who wants to borrow from you" (Matt. 5:38–42).*

You cannot read this portion of Matthew and come to any other conclusion—we must give **more** than is **asked** of us. We are **not** to resist any evil done to us—but we must not stop there. We must turn the other cheek; give the coat when he asks for our shirt; and go beyond one mile—instead we *must* go two. And when your reward comes, it will (more than likely) *not* come from your spouse, but will, instead, come directly from God!!

When my husband told me he was divorcing me, he told me that he was leaving all our debt to me. Debt I knew nothing about and what came from his involvement with the OW. In addition, though we had young children, he emphatically and unashamedly told me that he did not want to pay *any* child support whatsoever. The first time I was so distraught when he *said* he wouldn't pay, though praise God I didn't fight it and the first time, he did pay out of conviction even though the court didn't *make* him pay.

But, this time, rather than worry, I "enthusiastically" agreed to every one of his terms as he headed for his appointment with his attorney— but not before I gave him *more* than he asked for. Why? In order to follow the principle I just shared that Jesus taught us and this one in First Peter 3:8–9:

"To sum up, all of you be harmonious, sympathetic, brotherly, kindhearted, and humble in spirit; not returning evil for evil or insult for insult, but giving a blessing instead; for you were called for the very purpose that you might inherit a blessing."

The only debt he said he was going to take was a car payment. We had two cars, one was paid for, and the other still had payments. So I offered to take the one with payments since that was all that was left to *give* that he didn't already ask for. Several times he questioned me to be sure that was what I wanted to do, and then he happily agreed. I knew when he began that to agree to his terms was not enough, so as I was praying (while he was talking) to know what I could give as my extra mile, when, immediately, the car with the payments came to mind.

Shortly after my divorce that car was paid off and it has been such a blessing driving it because it reminds me of God's goodness, faithfulness, and His love! Years later even my mechanic tells me this car is blessed and anointed and seems to continue running supernaturally while it has become a classic other people admire. Yes, only by trusting God could this be true!!

As I mentioned, the first time my husband divorced me I was terrified at the thought of being an "accomplice" by signing the papers. But, since the terms of this divorce (the financial aspects) were so radical, as I said, my husband's attorney explained that the judge would never grant it without my signing the papers.

When I signed the papers, I had no idea what my financial state was. I simply trusted God. I knew that whatever was ahead, He knew about it (even if I didn't) and He would not only make a way *through* it, but the end would be a blessing!!

After I signed the papers, I realized that the amount of debt we had was really **three times** the amount that was stated in the divorce papers! From the time that my husband had become involved with the *AW our finances had begun to plummet that very month.

*I began referring to the OW as AW: The first time my husband having an OW hurt or "ouch" but this time due to the amount of His love I was able to feel, and knowing I was His bride, I was able to let go of fear and changed to calling her just "another woman" or AW.

Even though our church made a significant surge in new members and in donations early that year, a pile of personal and church debt began to incur! This is because this is a spiritual battle and His word tells us this:

*"For on account of a harlot one is **reduced** to a **loaf of bread**, and an adulteress hunts for the precious life" (Prov. 6:26).*

Because I had never been involved with paying our bills, or any part of the financial side of our church, I had to become totally dependent on God to lead me to know how to pay back the debt to the church and also be able to pay the bills that we had, and wasn't even sure if I knew *what* bills that had to be paid!!

Several times I got up in the middle of the night, when my children were asleep, so it would be quiet enough to seek God (and also so I was not interrupted), to begin to "seek and find" all the bills to get them into some sort of list, so I could get some sort of system to pay them.

My husband had a system all in his head; it was not in any organized fashioned, so I needed to search through our checkbooks (personal and church), search through our files (four drawers that were intermixed with other things he saved) to be able to even find all the bills so I could uncover all of our debt. To even know how to do this was a God thing! I really didn't know where to even begin, and often was on the verge of tears due to frustration, not fear—and yet, when I called upon my Husband, He was always there to comfort and take over!!

He led me to simply make a list of everything: the total that was due, how much it needed to be paid each month, when it was due, and out of which account I should be paying it. The Lord gave me such amazing wisdom!!! God showed me many things: one huge revelation was that, many bills our family was paying, should have been paid by the church. By paying from the church account, it would, in the end, save us thousands of dollars in taxes, since our church is nonprofit and doesn't pay taxes, and the bills were for church related things—but this came only *after* God set me up to look like a fool, so He alone would get the glory!!

The first two bills I paid were tithes to our church, and the other was to begin to pay off a building project that we (as a couple) had pledged to our church. My husband was gone (he left to go be with the AW), so I went ahead and paid that week's tithe, which caused us to be overdrawn in our personal account. The second one I paid out of the church account, that he told me, in anger, wiped out the donations we had received for a pledged project—he said the money was just not there and told me I was an idiot.

My husband was so angry that he kept telling our children that I was going to lose our house because I was so stupid. However, it was God who had set me up! Because of the accusations, I gained a greater dependence on the Lord to guide me and help me and to be my Lover. The results were incredible!!

God began to reveal so much financial wisdom to me, which totally blew my husband (and our children) away! Wisdom that could only be from God!! Rearranging who paid for each bill (church or family) was only the beginning. And, in addition, God surrounded me with favor wherever I turned— from that point on to the present!!

Favor like when we went to change the loan on the car into my name only (the one that I had used as my "extra mile" or as the "coat" He tells us to walk/give), the loan officer gave me a better rate, which dropped my monthly payments almost in half. My husband, who was there to sign the debt over to me, heard this and was shocked when the loan officer went onto say that I had a better credit rating than my husband did—only God could do that because I hadn't worked outside the home for years!!!

Then, the Lord took that incident to a higher blessing, when I was led to ask about rounding the payments *up* to be an even number, which I said would make it easier to write out the check each month, to which the loan officer stated would be fantastic, and said that it meant I would be paying more on the principal and it would be paid off almost a year earlier. This question totally baffled my husband because he *knows* I am a fool when it comes to financial issues! God got the glory!

1 Corinthians 1:27 (KJV), "But God hath chosen the foolish of the world to confound the wise."

1 Corinthians 1:27, "but God has chosen the *foolish* things of the world to confound the wise, and God has chosen the *weak* things of the world to shame the things which are strong."

When we were ready to transfer the title of the car, God set me up once again. The clerk we got ended up being a member of our church, who of course knew us (but not what was going on), and who ended up giving me favor again! Instead of it costing the $800 that it was supposed to cost to transfer the title, this woman wrote it up so it would cost *me* **nothing**!! Then she went even further and gave me two new license plates (one of our plates had been lost) and helped me pay for two years instead of one! Again, as I walked out—God got the glory!!

This happened over and over again over the next several weeks. Time after time the Lord would give me wisdom and surround me with favor! And it only got better *after* the divorce was final!! God was showing me, my husband, my children, and everyone else, how much He loved me (by how He kept blessing me) and that I truly was His bride and He was my Husband. Dear Reader, the same will happen to you when you accept the Lord's proposal and become His bride ladies.

*"For your **husband** is your Maker, Whose name is the **LORD** of hosts; and your Redeemer is the Holy One of Israel, Who is called the God of all the earth" (Is. 54:5).*

But you must expect trials and more debt when you trust the Lord to provide! During these same days, while awaiting the final divorce decree, my car turned up with a "check engine" light coming on (not good). And once again, because of my "enthusiastic" giving to my husband, he offered to take the car in for me so I could keep my date with my children to go to a water park. Walking out these principles work dear reader!!

When my husband called, he said that the mechanic found that I needed some servicing done, but that I did not need a repair (praise the Lord!). So my husband asked me what I wanted to do (he knew that I was in utter financial ruin and had *no* money to pay for anything). Though I had a "twinge" of fear that pricked my heart, I quickly sent up a "flair prayer" while he was explaining about the servicing needed (that I didn't understand anyway!). God reminded me that **He** was my Husband now, and of course—He would pay for *anything* that I needed!

So I quickly answered, "Go ahead!" to everything that needed servicing (since my husband had been involved with the AW for months, and our finances were plummeting months, so he had to neglect things, like keeping the car serviced). Though he hesitated he said, "Okay" but I could tell again he thought I was making a huge mistake.

A few hours later, my husband called to tell me "some amazing news!" He said that the manufacturer of my car now provided a new service plan for cars built the year mine was built and the years prior, and that it would always be the same fee each time I had it serviced— no matter what was needed!! Not only was I shocked, so was my husband, whose car (the one that was paid for) just missed this new service plan. Ladies, this again is God!!

Our beloved Husband actually looks for opportunities to remind us (and even our earthly husbands or ex-husbands) that He is able to provide all of our needs!!! Don't miss an opportunity to turn to your new Husband when a need arises so that you don't miss any blessing!

And men, God says He is your provider too! You need to get a hold of this since too many men think they need to work hard in order to provide for their families. If you are in financial ruin, first be sure you are not in adultery, since this is ultimately the source of most financial ruin. This goes for pornography too since Jesus said clearly this is adultery in Matthew 5:28, "but I say to you that everyone who looks at a woman with lust for her has already committed adultery with her in his heart."

Men, if your heart is clear, then claim this verse so that God will provide everything you, your wife, and your children need:

Psalm 127:2 says clearly, "It is vain for you to rise up early, to retire late, to eat the bread of painful labors; for He gives to His beloved even in his sleep."

And Psalm 37:25 says, "I have been young and now I am old, yet I have not seen the righteous forsaken or his descendants begging bread."

If you are struggling financially it is either due to adultery, another sin, OR because you are trying to provide yourself, not looking to God to do it for you. And God wants to go beyond to supplying needs, but to shower you with blessings!

One of my absolute favorite blessings was how He blessed me with a new wedding ring, which is in the next chapter. But before I share that awesome testimony with you, let me share one more very important principle.

# Chapter 11

# The Danger of a Poverty Mentality

*"For the mouth speaks out of that
which fills the heart."*
*—Matthew 12:34*

So many women, men, and especially those who are the heads of their households fall into what I describe as the "Poverty Mentality." Large families are plagued with it. The Poverty Mentality is basically when the phrase, "I can't afford it" takes over a person's vocabulary and soon enters their heart.

*"For the mouth speaks out of that which fills the heart"* (Matthew 12:34).

It is so easy to fall into this mindset and mental stronghold, especially when you pay the bills and begin to take over the finances, or are now trying to "get by" with one income instead of two. It can hit when you look at what your divorce papers say you are going to get or what you are going to have to pay, or like me, when you total up your family's debt hoping to consolidate your loans you didn't apply for but are responsible to pay.

Yet this is a trap from the enemy because it is contrary to Scripture and who our Father is. I am not trying to be "spiritually weird" here and encourage us to all go out and buy whatever we want because our spiritual "Sugar Daddy" will pay for it! But let's not be like the world, and *worry* about how we will make it financially, when the Bible promises that He will take care of **all** not just **some** of our needs!

*"And my God will supply **all your needs** according to His riches in glory in Christ Jesus" (Philippians 4:19).*

If we can believe God for our salvation, then why not believe God for our financial needs, wants, and for the blessings He longs to give us?

*"Therefore the LORD **longs to be gracious** to you, and therefore He waits on high to have compassion on you For the LORD is a God of justice; how blessed are all those who long for Him" (Isaiah 30:18).*

God says that without faith, it is impossible to please Him (Hebrews 11:6). So we keep telling everyone, "We can't afford it" or "I don't know how we are going to make it," it is like a slap in the face to our heavenly Father!

How would you feel if your son or daughter went around telling friends or went to school telling everyone that they didn't know if they would be able to have a lunch the next week? Or saying you couldn't afford buy them the shoes that they needed? How would you feel if they shamed you like that? And what would people think of you, when you of course, would be able to provide for your own child?

It is the same way when you shame your heavenly Father and/or Husband. When you shame Him by telling people that though you are a child of God (that you profess to everyone) or the bride of the

Lord of Hosts, but, He is unable or unwilling to provide for what you need; that you can barely make it and you don't know where you will get enough money. This has to be a painful slap in the face to the One whom you profess to love and trust.

And maybe you don't go around *telling* everyone, you keep it to yourself, but your appearance shouts it to everyone! Your clothes are old because you haven't bought any new clothes in years. You let the roots grow out in your hair, or don't have your hair cut often enough. You're car is full of trash and the outside is dirty. You let your appearance go, since you have told yourself you don't have enough money for shoes for your children. You are the picture of poverty, when you have a heavenly Father and/or Husband who has **all** that you need and wants to provide if you would just trust Him!

You need to take care of what you have (including your appearance): your home, your lawn, your car (inside and out), and your children. And when you have a need, or even a want, simply ask God the Father or your Heavenly Husband for it. He is just waiting for you to ask! He wants to bless you with good things, as long as you take care of what He gives you and He only asks that you give Him all the praise, by telling others how awesome He is! If do that, soon you will find people you know will also so want a relationship with Him too! But most Christians tend forget Who it was who gave the blessing to them since they focus on *earning* money rather than just allowing God to do what He said He would do!

*". . . you may say in your heart, 'My power and the strength of my hand made me this wealth.' But you shall remember the LORD your God, for it is He who **is giving you power to make wealth**, that He may confirm His covenant which He swore to your fathers, as it is this day" (Deuteronomy 8:17–18).*

If a person believes they are poor, their countenance, appearance, and what they say will reflect poverty. Yet, if a person believes they are rich (according to His riches in Christ Jesus) then their countenance, appearance, and everything that they say will radiate wealth!

My ex-husband used to get so irritated because I always told everyone that we were "rich!" It all began years ago when I saw a very tall black man trying to sell some pecans in a fast food hamburger restaurant so he could buy something to eat. When they said at the counter, no they weren't interested, I went up to the counter and asked if I could buy him a meal. He said, "No, that's okay" after looking at me then looking down at the floor. So out of my mouth comes, "Well, my husband is very rich, and he would want me to buy you something to eat." So I paid for it and sat down. (Saying we were rich was not a lie; in comparison to what this man had—we *were* very rich!)

When the man got his tray of food, he walked up and asked if he could sit with me. I could smell that he reeked of alcohol and urine, but I said, "Please do." Without looking up he asked me, "Why did you do that? Why did you buy me this food?" I told him that God had sent me there because he was hungry, and God just wanted him to know that He loved him. I said that I was on my way to church for a revival that night, and really wasn't hungry, but felt I was to come in and get something to eat. And when I saw him, I knew why I had come.

The man asked me about the revival and said he would go to church with me. I said that there were no strings attached, and that he didn't need to go. But he said that if I were willing to take him, he would come.

Since I was late, I knew there would be no parking (only blocks away), but when I got there, I noticed a spot right in the front. When I walked in with this heavily soiled black man, you would have thought I had entered with a king! The ushers came over and gave him a royal welcome and found a seat for "him" near the front. And guess what? This man was the first person who ran to the altar and wept to accept Jesus that night!! I, on the other hand, was "reprimanded by the head usher" for my foolishness and the danger I had put myself in.

My husband and children, too, made me promise I would never do that again. Yet, I am grateful to God that He thought me worthy to help in saving that man's soul and helping Him find peace.

Our finances and wealth are not so we can store up riches on earth, but so that we can be used by God (in big and small ways) to advance His kingdom. But unless you are faithful in small things, especially in your lack (right now), then you will never receive the wealth that He wants to entrust to you!

*"And the one also who had received the one talent came up and said, 'Master, I knew you to be a hard man, reaping where you did not sow and gathering where you scattered no seed.*

*And I was afraid, and went away and hid your talent in the ground. See, you have what is yours.' But his master answered and said to him, 'you wicked, lazy slave, you knew that I reap where I did not sow and gather where I scattered no seed.*

*Then you ought to have put my money in the bank, and on my arrival I would have received my money back with interest. Therefore take away the talent from him, and give it to the one who has the ten talents. For to everyone who has, more shall be given, and he will have an abundance; but from the one who does not have, even what he does have shall be taken away" (Matthew 25:24–29).*

Since my divorce, I have never had more money in my pocket or more financial blessings to use for His kingdom in big and small ways! God saw my heart (by my actions and what I said) when faced with financial ruin this time and He continues to reward me according to my faith in Him!

Even after the divorce papers had been signed, and I had taken all our debt (and more than what my husband had asked for), my ex-husband approached *me* for "a loan." I told him that he could take anything he wanted, and it was not a loan, but a gift. I told him to just give me a few minutes to balance my checkbook so that he (not I) could see what I had available and told him to take all of it if he wanted to. I told him that he knew, above what I knew, what I would need to pay the bills (since he had been the one paying them for years).

Later, when I looked at the checkbook, I was shocked because asked for two-thirds of what I had in our accounts (that he was no longer on; he had taken me to the bank to take himself off, I would not have asked him to get off). I quickly wrote the check and handed it to him. He just said, "Thanks."

Thankfully, our blessings don't return to us *from* our husbands or ex-husbands—they come from the Lord! Ladies, almost immediately God blessed me beyond my wildest dreams!!!! Within a few minutes after leaving, my ex-husband called and told me that I could have **all** our frequent flier miles he had accumulated, allowing me, for the first time to travel.

When our frequent flier miles had been discussed right after the divorce was first filed, the Lord prompted me to ask if I could have "just *one* trip" which may have prompted him giving them to me after I generously gave him the money he needed. The amazing thing is, my ex-husband told me he guessed that we probably had about two and a half trips of earned flying miles. But because of how enthusiastically agreeable I had been by signing the papers and all his other demands, he said that I could have them all.

So right after the "loan" that I gave him as a "gift" (remember, I told him he never needed to pay me back), and after he had offered them to me, he checked to see how many miles I would use up for each domestic trip. Both of us were totally in shock when I had **five** trips on one card and **two** on another—7 trips would cost me nothing!!! I sensed my ex really struggling, wanting to ask for some miles back, but because of God's perfect timing, and Him wanting to bless my faith in Him, my ex-husband never asked, and I kept quiet!

"Even a fool, when he keeps silent, is considered wise. When he closes his lips he is counted as prudent" (Proverbs 17:28).

For two years, I used those miles to be able to visit people as He prompted me, due to the lovingkindness of the Lord, my new Husband, who wanted to bless me because I simply trusted Him!

And in case you are wondering why I didn't offer the flying miles back to my ex when I heard him struggling, it was because the full principle, as I mentioned, is to give more when *asked* and he never asked!

**This is one reason you (and even I) have much less than we would have if we would simply ***ask*** and, how we wouldn't be taken advantage of it we waited until we were ***asked*** before we offered.

Since I have a limited amount of pages left in this book, you will have to read my upcoming book *Breaking Free from The Poverty Mentality"* for all the principles and testimonies I've accumulated from others as I shared my story with them. But let me at least tell you that simply "asking" was such a revelation for me, which happened right before my divorce.

Just months *before* I knew my divorce was about to divorce me, while watching a television show, I saw gorgeous a front load washer and drier, and I told my Husband about them. That's when He said, "Why don't you just ask Me?" I said, "Okay, I am asking!!" and immediately my old washer started making noise! I got so excited and told my husband that it meant that I was going to be blessed by Him giving me the one that I had seen on television. His comment was, "It just means we need a repair man stupid!"

Just months after my divorce I did get a gorgeous front load washer and drier, in black, which were a dream for me!! And every time I see them, I think of His love and goodness to me—which has been passed on to the next generation! Soon after my son married, I blessed him with these (due to his growing family) and see how my daughter-in-law also thanks the Lord each time she throws in a load of laundry!

Dear reader, whatever you do or don't do will be passed on through generations. So read this and claim it in your heart, not just for you, but for your children and grandchildren and generations to come!

The Spirit of the Lord God is upon me,
Because the Lord has anointed me
To bring good news to the afflicted;
He has sent me to bind up the brokenhearted,
To proclaim liberty to captives,
And freedom to prisoners;
To proclaim the favorable year of the Lord,
And the day of vengeance of our God;
To comfort all who mourn,
To grant those who mourn in Zion,
Giving them a garland instead of ashes,
The oil of gladness instead of mourning,
The mantle of praise instead of a spirit of fainting.
So they will be called oaks of righteousness,
The planting of the Lord,
that HE MAY BE GLORIFIED.
Then they will rebuild the ancient ruins,
They will raise up the former devastations,
And they will repair the ruined cities,
The desolations of many **generations**.
—Isaiah 61:1–4

# Chapter 12

# Watch Out for Fear

*"Do not **fear** their intimidation, and do not be troubled"*
*—1 Peter 3:13-15*

*"But **seeing** the wind, he became afraid"*
*—Matthew 14:30*

Obedience to follow His principles is *impossible* when it's combined with fear. Fear, which will always want to come in to stop you from gaining all that God has for you! Let me share another faith building testimony to show how God *longs* to be gracious to us!

*"[God Is **Gracious** and Just] Therefore the LORD **longs** to be **gracious** to you, and therefore He waits on high to have compassion on you For the LORD is a God of justice; how blessed are all those who long for Him" (Isaiah 30:18).*

When I took over the finances, one of the areas of debt that I was the most concerned about was a building pledge we (my husband and I) had made almost two years earlier that I *knew* was almost due to be paid off. For some reason, back when we made it, I felt that there was something very significant in our making this particular pledge.

How did I know? Because my husband really balked and resisted "even praying" about making the pledge in the first place; he argued with me about it, though I never said a word, but when he kept pressing me, my only response was, "Can you just pray about it?" when he asked me what I thought.

"A gentle *answer* turns away wrath, but harsh words stir up anger" (Proverbs 15:1).

Dear reader, any time you see resistance like that, which is out of proportion to what is being discussed, you can be sure that the enemy is lurking about, trying to steal something from you (or your family or your ministry). And you can't blame any loss on your spouse (or ex-spouse), boss or parent, since *you* have the power to keep and gain every blessing through *your* obedience and trust in the Lord! And if someone does try to steal something from you that is when you really can **rejoice** since God promises a double recompense!

Isaiah 61:7-9 says, "Instead of your shame you will have a **double** portion, and instead of humiliation they will shout for joy over their portion therefore they will possess a **double** portion in their land, everlasting joy will be theirs. For I, the LORD, love justice, **I hate robbery** in the burnt offering; and **I will** faithfully give them their recompense"!

After my husband *finally* prayed, he had an ***immediate*** change of heart and excitement. He said he knew now how important it was to pledge—and it was far *more* than I would have ever dreamed we would give!! However, because I was never included in the finances, I was totally in the dark as to how much we had paid on the pledge (paying it down each month over the two years as the church says we are to do). When the announcement was made in church, that the pledges would be due within a few short weeks, it was during the time of my husband divorcing me and had already turned the finances over to me.

When I asked my husband how much we still owed, my husband said he didn't know, but that I could call the church accountant for the balance. To my surprise, three-fourths (thousands of dollars!!) were still due! For me to pay this would truly *have to* come from God—I would need *Him* to make a way.

The significance in this pledge was confirmed over, and over, and over again when time after time, my husband kept trying to persuade me *not* to pay it. He told me that he had made the pledge, not me, so I didn't need to pay it. He said I should contact the pastor who was over the single moms and widows to ask to be released from the commitment! He told my children that if I acted so stupidly, I would surely lose our home, so they, too, began to beg me not to pay it. However, for me, each attempt to stop me confirmed that to miss paying this would be a huge loss for me and for our future in regard to our finances.

Let me add something here: each time my husband spoke to me, we were still legally married, but since he had moved out and filed for divorce, he kept telling me that I needed to make the decision myself (that he was only concerned and didn't want me to make a mistake that would mean losing our house—remember I told you it was a very large amount!). And each time, I assured him that I would do nothing but pray about it, which I did. And each time I did, God continued to tell me that He wanted me to pay it and He would show me the way.

That is the other point I want to make—there was no way that I could have found a way to pay it. I was backed up so far to the Red Sea to the point that my heels were getting wet! God had to be the One to do it, which I kept assuring my husband and children—there was no way I could do it, but **if** He wanted it paid, He would make a way.

The day that the pledge was due—came and went. God didn't show me a way to pay it, but when I prayed, I still believed God wanted me to seek Him to pay it even if it was late! Then one evening, our senior pastor made an announcement, "Anyone who had not yet paid is *released* from what you owe!" Yet, when I prayed and asked if that was *Him* speaking to me, He, again, assured me that He would make a way for me to pay it!

Almost a month after the pledges were due, God showed me a way!! I was so excited to write the check, my hands trembled with excitement. Yet I needed to wait three more days for our prayer meeting so I could put it in the offering! And even then, only two minutes before I was to slip the envelope into the offering, the enemy had a dear friend lean forward to tell me something to steal the joy I was experiencing, as I watched the offering plate coming down my row!!

But PRAISE THE LORD!! God got the victory, **and less than three hours later**, God blessed me beyond my dreams!! Even now my eyes fill with tears when I think of how awesome God is!!

Just a little over two hours after I put the check in the offering, I got an email from a friend who had moved to the east coast who said that God had laid it on her heart to "Sow a substantial seed" into my ministry to women!! The seed was the EXACT amount of the *entire* pledge!!! Not just what I had put in the offering just two and a half hours earlier, but ALL that we gave over the two years—the *entire* pledge!

But that is not the end of the blessing—when I called and told my children, they in turn told their father, who called me and left me a message on my cell phone: "You were right Michele, and I was dead wrong" and he went on to tell me he was so happy for me. This was huge (as I am sure it would be for you too)!!!!

**The Blessings Continue Long After the Divorce**

Almost a year to the day that my husband announced that he was divorcing me, I was able to go the extra mile that has opened the door for me to lead countless people to know the Lord. It is so absurd, however, that many Christians believe I am completely nuts. Nevertheless, it is the lost souls who need Him, right? So I am glad that the Lord provided these outrageous testimonies that have proved to shake up those who hear them.

When my husband was leaving, he did his best to try to help me get a handle on the finances by advising me to consolidate our debt by taking out a second loan on our home. Since I was simply following the Lord's leading, it never came to mind until I began to travel extensively out of the country. While gone for long periods, it was difficult to pay so many different bills, so the Lord led me to look into a consolidation loan so I could pay off most of our debt, leaving me with a lower percentage rate and only one bill instead of dozens.

It was on the last day before I signed the papers that I got a call from a woman (my neighbor and friend) who told me some shocking news. In the midst of the divorce, my divorce papers were written up in a way that it said that I had a huge "judgment" against me. My husband did not only ask to pay no child support, and leave all the debt to me, but he wanted half of the equity in our home. So his attorney told him the only way he would get it (since the divorce judge would never agree to it) was to file a judgment against me for half the equity. God saw fit to back me into the Red Sea *again*. A huge judgment against me meant that financially it ruined me— even worse than a bankruptcy would do (since a judgment stays on your record for ten years not just seven like a bankruptcy).

My friend (who was handling my consolidation loan) asked me to call my ex-husband since he could easily get this *amended* through his attorney and allow me to pay it when I refinanced the house. Immediately my husband agreed, but a day later told me that his attorney told him NOT to do so since that was the only way he was sure he would get his money. I gently reminded him of how I had given him *more* than he asked for when he filed for divorce, had given him rather than loaned him money, and that this should prove that I would do the same thing when the house was refinanced.

Nevertheless, he said he had prayed about it and God said not to do it.

"Then the LORD said to Moses, 'Go to Pharaoh, for **I have hardened his heart** and the heart of his servants, that I may perform these signs of Mine among them'" (Exodus 10:1).

Christians are notorious for always giving the enemy the credit for a disaster or for causing us difficulty, when it often times is God who wants to do something special in the life of the believer when we are willing to be used by Him and not protect ourselves or fight back!

"...not returning evil for evil, or insult for insult, but giving a blessing instead; for you were *called* for the **very purpose that you might inherit a blessing**" (1 Peter 3:9).

When my ex-husband adamanetly refused to amend the judgment, I told my friend what he said, which led to a very surprising offer from the loan company. They said that if I were to take out another loan and pay off my ex-husband five years early, then they would put the first loan through. Immediately it sounded like God since He tells us that we need to bless our enemies, and to give my ex-husband a huge lump sum five years early would certainly be a blessing!

Since this was such a big step, I told my friend to give me 24 hours to seek the Lord; however, immediately the Lord brought the answer to me in the form of another surprising situation. My son came in and sat next to me with his laptop and asked me how things were going. I told him that I was seeking God about the judgment payout and told him my only hesitancy was something that had happened a few months earlier. I was about to bless my ex-husband with a much smaller sum of money, but my children had stopped me and begged me not to. When I asked why, they said they were concerned that he would use the money to move back to our area. They no longer trusted him and were afraid that he would flaunt his new lifestyle, and show up at the mall, or a restaurant with his girlfriend that they would have to explain to their friends.

To my surprise, my son said that they no longer were worried about their father using the money to move closer. A bit baffled how he knew that for sure, he went on to say that his dad just announced he was engaged to his high school sweetheart that he had left us for. I thanked my son profusely since I now had my answer—give my ex-husband the huge lump sum of money early.

"But I say to you, do not resist an evil person; but whoever slaps you on your right cheek, turn the other to him also. If anyone wants to sue you and take your shirt, let him have your coat also. Whoever forces you to go one mile, go with him two. Give to him who asks of you, and do not turn away from him who wants to borrow from you" (Matthew 5:38).

Then, that same night I woke up at midnight with the most absurd, outrageous thought that I told God had to be Him (because a thought like what I was thinking would never enter my mind), but just to be sure, I would dismiss it and just go back to sleep. If it was Him, I asked that He confirm it in the morning.

When I woke up the absurdity doubled, with a more of a plan of what He was now asking me to do. I didn't need to wait any later than 8 in the morning (when I knew my ex-husband would be awake) to step forward and state the outrageous way He showed me He wanted me to do. When I telephoned, I began by telling him that the next day he would be getting a certified check for the full amount of half the equity of our home sent by special courier. He was so stunned he couldn't even speak, but then he tried to thank me over and over, and also apologize at the same time for not signing the papers to release me and that he knew there was a distinct possibly that I may never recover my financial ruin done by the judgment he placed on me.

I told him that it was okay, and "you're welcome." Then I went on to share with him what the Lord spoke to me in the middle of the night, and then again, with even more details that morning. I said, "I heard *congratulations* are in order. I heard you are engaged!" He mumbled, "Yes, sorry, I had planned to tell you myself." I told him it was not a problem, and that I wanted to do something special to bless him and his fiancé with a really special honeymoon.

Again he went silent, so I continued to tell him that I had quite a few new flying miles, and that they would take him and his new bride just about anywhere in the world, except Africa. (I explained these were the miles that I was going to use to visit a friend in Africa with me, but I was short flying miles.) Then I completed the honeymoon package gift with a week at a resort since I also got in the divorce a crown level timeshare that they could use (he didn't want the timeshare because there were ongoing payments due, but what the Lord helped me pay off!). Though he tried not to accept, he finally gave in and again thanked me over and over.

Ladies, I wasn't doing this to impress him or you or anyone else. What I did was God's plan, that's all. And why, you may ask, would God want to bless a man who committed adultery, who left his family and had just ruined a family's financial credit (amongst many other things)? Because, you may remember, it was while we were yet sinners, yes, sinners, that He laid down His life and died for us. This principle is as powerful today as it was back then.

When I shared this with ladies in Nairobi, Kenya one of their top female leaders couldn't get over it and told the audience that if it were her, and her husband had done the same thing to her, she would have found the largest object she could find and beat him with it! But then she said, "God help us all to have the humility that is possible with a relationship that Michele has with our Savior."

Again, this is not about me; I am no superstar (or maybe you just think I more of a nut or a fool), but I believe that God is looking for anyone, just someone, who is willing to be used by Him to prove that He is as amazing as He really is!

What is exciting is that I have shared this story with several strangers on the phone (when closing credit card accounts as they got paid off, and because these were my ex-husband's accounts that I was paying off and closing, I was easily able to share my faith with them too because they *asked* why I did what I did). Most of them told me this was not the God they had ever heard of at all, and asked me what it all meant, so I often spent almost an hour sharing about the Husband I had now and that the church (anyone who accepted His gift of eternal life) was His bride.

One of my favorite responses was the cab driver in Hong Kong who slammed on his brakes, turned around and **shouted** at me: "Why did you do that?! Why did you do that?!!!" My response was simple, "Because while we were yet sinners, Jesus died for us." His response, "This Jesus is Someone I need to know. Please tell me about Him." This is what witnessing to someone is about. When they witness your peace in the midst of horrible horrendous storms, only then do they beg to know Him too!

As I close this chapter, I hope that everything that I have shared with you will give you the faith to trust the Lord with everything and anything that is going on now and in your future!

When facing divorce, it doesn't matter what your spouse wants, just be sure to *give* **more** than he/she *asks*. It doesn't matter if there are lies your spouse is telling you or there are lies in the divorce papers. It doesn't matter if your spouse tries to steal from you, or if the other person in your spouse's life (or parents or the other man/woman) who has put your spouse up to it—bless him/her by giving your coat! God is your Source! If you look to Him and give all you have when asked (and then more), then God will open the windows of heaven over your life too!

You may even see a deadline come and go, but God is not bound by deadlines or death!! He often waits, like He did with Lazarus (when he waited for him to be in the tomb 3 days and began to stink) before He shows up in your situation!

And if you have other people who can help you financially (I don't, so that it does not pose a temptation), do **not** go to them for help!! Everyone, but God, has a *limited* supply and there are always strings attached. Don't sell yourself short! Tap into God who has it all and is more generous (and loving) than any other person ever created!!

**Update:** God bless me in so many ways, more than double! One blessing that happened a year after I gave my ex-husband the honeymoon to Hawaii. I was able to bless my son with a destination wedding in Kauai, Hawaii— with a honeymoon— a full week at a gorgeous beachside resort.

# Chapter 13

# A Symbol of My Love

*"My Beloved is mine, and I am His"*
*—Song of Solomon 2:16*

When I knew that the divorce was going to go through this time, knowing He had been preparing me, and it was God's *perfect* plan for my life, I knew that I was going to need a new set of wedding rings. So I began to ask the Lord to show me what He had planned for me to wear.

First, I was led to explain it to my husband, reminding him of RMI's principles: that once we were divorced, I would no longer wear the wedding rings he gave me, but would purchase another set to wear. And that the reason I was going to continue to wear a wedding ring after the divorce, was to show others that I was *not* available, and that I was not interested in attracting another man.

Though I was "reminding" my husband of the principles (that he basically knew since I led Bible RYM and WW Bible studies five years in our church), I would encourage you to share this and other principles with your spouse when times like these surfaces. Basically, explaining that you are learning through "a ministry you joined" without telling him/her that your desire, if it is, to restore your marriage. You, too, can tell your spouse that the ministry is helping you understand the mistakes *you* made in the marriage, and that you're taught never to look at what your spouse was doing or are doing. And that one of the ministry's goals is to help the person become a better marriage partner so that their separation and/or divorce is a better experience for their spouse or ex-spouse than the marriage was for them." Much more of this is covered in RMI's Be Encouraged videos that I would encourage you to get and watch over and over again as I did. Had it not been for me watching them as often as I did, I am sure I could not have done a fraction had Erin not laid a foundation for us to travel on and build on to.

Unlike the first time I faced divorce, the Lord showed me this time when facing divorce, that I was always to take the *offensive* rather than the defensive position whenever I could, which is why He led me to explain to my husband that I would not be wearing his wedding rings after the divorce. Taking the offensive, as I mentioned earlier, does **not** mean being aggressive, but taking the *spiritually* offensive, rather than a spiritually *defensive* position (cowering or hiding due to fearing what is coming next). I needed to step forward, as the Lord led, whenever He opened the door for me. He reminded me that we are the "head and not the tail" and brought this verse to my mind:

*"The LORD will make you the head and not the tail, and you only will be above, and you will not be underneath, if you listen to the commandments of the LORD your God, which I charge you today, to observe them carefully" (Deuteronomy 28:13).*

Dear reader, when you speak to your spouse about continuing to wear a set of wedding rings, not the ones representing your marriage with them, it **may** set you up for your spouse to tell you that you need to date, find someone yourself, and move on. And if you are not spiritually and emotionally prepared, it can be very painful! So be sure you spend a lot of time being loved by the Lord, (possibly fast) and continue telling the Lord that **He is** all you want, **He is** all you need, that (ladies) **He is** your Husband, and *you are* His bride! Say it over and over again every day while asking the Lord to open the opportunity to speak to your husband about your rings.

"Who is there to harm you if you prove zealous for what is good? But even if you should suffer for the sake of righteousness, you are blessed and do not fear their intimidation, and do not be troubled, but sanctify Christ as Lord in your hearts, always being ready to make a defense to everyone who asks you to give an account for the hope that is in you, yet with gentleness and reverence" (1 Peter 3:13-15).

Before I spoke to my husband, the Lord reminded me that the gold wedding band that I wore, I had actually purchased myself. Right after our restoration, my husband had given me a thin wedding band, but it broke several times (which later, after my divorce, I felt *may* have been a sign of broken vows and promises?). One time when picking it up from our jeweler, the man told me that I needed to purchase one of *their* rings that they guaranteed would never break. I purchased it, and never broke again!

So when the Lord opened the door for me to share about wearing my rings, I told him that even though we were in the midst of getting a divorce, that I would wear the set he had given me until the divorce was final, then switch to a new set.

I told him that since I had bought the band myself that I would continue to wear the wedding and then find some sort of diamond (probably something not real) to wear with it. Then, I knew what was coming next—he told me I needed to find someone new! But because I was prepared, I was able to explain (again) that I was so happy now, that I had proven (to myself) that I had not been a good wife to him (so why should I subject anyone else having to have me as a wife), and that I wanted to be able to devote my love and my time to our children.

But before he entered into the "moving on" suggestion, because I took the offensive position and approached him about his permission to continue to wear my rings until the divorce was final, and then to switch to a new set, he told me that he wouldn't mind if I wore "his" rings forever. I thanked him but told him it would probably be better for me to remove it and put it in our safe deposit box. I am sure by rejecting his offer, he was hurt and wanted to hurt me back. So when that thought came to mind, rather than retreat or cringe, I told the Lord I needed Him to get me ready.

In the meantime, just a few weeks later, after praying about where I would find the ring He had for me, I envisioned a local department and I assumed He was showing me the $10 rings that looked so real. I thought how great, and planned to pick up at least two, maybe three of them, to wear depending on the occasion. I figured that women don't really remember other women's settings, so this would work out really well.

When I got there, I found only one ring that would work as a wedding ring, but even though it said it was my size, it just did *not* fit. For a brief second my heart sank. I knew I did not have the time to shop for a ring. So I began to pray in the Spirit asking Him to show me where my ring was, and immediately I spotted a beautiful ring in a case that was marked 85% off.

Though it was beautiful and fit me perfectly, I still hesitated to buy a ring like that for myself. But then the saleswoman spoke up and said that I had 90 days to return it if I didn't want it. So, in faith, I purchased it, but told my children who were with me that I was probably *not* going to keep it. When all of a sudden, I remembered that I needed to pick up some printing for an upcoming Bible study.

This however, did make me cringe after I had just paid for my ring, since I knew the printing was for a large group of about 200 women who had signed up. When I got there, just about to pay for the copies, seeing the huge amount I was about to pay for, the sales lady said, "Oh, wait…There used to be a code I put in for our 'valued' customers, months ago, that took 15% off the price." I said, "Well, why not try" knowing that 15% would save me a LOT of money!

When she hit the key, I saw the price drop by **the exact amount that my ring cost**!! I had saved the same amount of money that I had just spent only a few minutes earlier for my ring!! In other words—my ring cost me nothing!! What a confirmation from the Lord that He wanted me to have it!

When I hurried to the car, I told my children what had just happened, and then drove to my older son's apartment so that he and his roommate could see the ring and hear how it happened. Funny thing too, my son asked me three times to repeat the story and said, "Wow, this is so God, Mom!"

But the really awesome thing about this blessing was what it did for me while waiting to hear that the divorce was final. Instead of dreading or fearing when the divorce would be final, I instead couldn't wait for it to be final because all I could think about was wearing my new ring!! How's that for God??? Though at times fear would put a tiny twinge in my stomach or in my heart, for the most part, there was only excitement and anticipation for when I would be able to begin wearing my new ring!

I thanked the Lord over and over: all day long, when I went to bed, and when I woke up. I thought the day the divorce would be final, and I could wear my new ring would *never* arrive!

Then, one day my husband was hanging around me in the kitchen and was acting kind of strange. When I headed to my bedroom, he followed me in and said that he needed to tell me something. Immediately I confess, I excitedly interrupted and said, "Oh, did you hear from your attorney? Is the divorce final?" He bowed his head and said yes that he had heard the news the day before. To which I replied excitedly, "Really? Oh, that means I get to wear my new ring, did you see it?!" as he followed me to my walk-in closet. I opened the box, took off my ring, put the rings he had given me in the same box and slipped my ring on to show to him.

While he was looking at it, dumbfounded, I asked him if he had heard how I had gotten it. He said that he "sort of had," but would I tell him? I did (just as I told you above), and then he looked at it again more closely. He said, "Michele, not only is it incredible how you got it, but a ring like that should have cost you about eight thousand dollars!!" Dear reader, this is how much your Husband longs to bless you!!! This is how much He loves you and me!!

"Therefore the LORD longs to be gracious to you, and therefore He WAITS on high to have compassion on you. For the LORD is a God of justice; how blessed are all those who long for Him" (Isaiah 30:18).

The reason I took the time to write all of this down is not just so you can praise the Lord for how awesome He is, but to give you just *one* example of how He wants to bless you when you, too, seek Him as your Husband!

The ring story does not end there. When my husband took me out on a "lunch date" (those were his words), just before he was about to leave to move states away, he took my hand and just stared at my ring and tears filled his eyes. I am not sure exactly what he was thinking, but God not only used my rings to bless me and help me feel loved and not rejected (because I followed His principles and then sought His plan for how to replace what I was to wear in their place), but He used them in my ex-husband's life in *some* way (maybe regret for the choices he had made; who, but God knows and it's not something I dwell on).

Before I end this chapter, I want you to know that the enemy is always lurking around to *steal* your joy, or to bring pain to your blessing.

John 10:10 tells us clearly that "The thief comes only to *steal* and kill and destroy; I came that they may have life, and have it abundantly."

And First Peter 5:8 warns us to always be ready, "Be of *sober* spirit, be on the alert your adversary, the devil, prowls around like a roaring lion, seeking someone to devour."

When my ex-husband saw that I had put my wedding ring from him in the box, he said before leaving my room that he would bring *his ring* over to put in the safe deposit box too, since "he didn't *want* it." But I took the "enthusiastic" response and said, "Oh, great, I think I have another ring box right here!" But the enemy was determined to keep using his hurt to hurt me back, so then my ex-husband said, "Oh, I will bring my sapphire ring over and put it in there too since I won't be wearing it" referring to the ring I gave him as a wedding gift when we married. I was still able to enthusiastically say, "Oh, why not offer it to one of the boys?" This obviously hurt, so he dropped subject by saying that the boys would *not* be interested.

The next day, the battle to hurt me continued, as he handed me both rings, along the first letter I sent him that he kept in his top drawer, which also had a picture of me in it. I was able to stay strong and enthusiastic, opening it to tell him I would save the picture, then walked over and threw my letter to him in the trash. I didn't do it to be mean, but just as a sign that it did not affect me (and as a silent message to my new Husband that I would be forever faithful to Him). However, the horror on his face told me what he was feeling in his heart. I was able to take to all the rings to the safe deposit box at the bank the next day, and though the enemy tried several times to hurt me, because it hurt my ex-husband, he wanted to hurt me back, but the enemy was never able to steal my joy.

Dear reader, you may see things like this on television, when each is trying to hurt the other, but I will tell you honestly, I would never ever try to hurt my ex-husband, but fight only to keep what Jesus died to give me. He promised that "perfect love casts out all fear" and that we are to be careful not to allow the enemy to steal the abundant life He died to give us. I knew to prove my love to my Savior, my Beloved, and my new Husband, I needed to do so just as I did, but was only able to do so by His grace and the love I felt from Him!

Every morning I am just as excited to put my new ring on, and many times throughout the day, I feel so blessed that the Lord chose me as His bride. There is no shame when you give God your life and trust Him to this level of walking with Him radically and enthusiastically.

Amazing, too, is that my ex-husband was more in love, and more drawn to me that any man who had ever just divorced his wife! Again, it is not because I am anyone special, because I'm not. It is because I am willing to trust the Lord enough to not just walk along this journey He has chosen for me, but walk it with *enthusiasm* and excitement! Is there any other way we should walk hand-in-hand with our Savior?

Here are more testimonies that prove that this can happen to you too!!

## "My New Ring"

I am so EXCITED!!! I have a BEAUTIFUL New Ring to wear. For a few months now I have had this desire for a rose gold ring. I have been talking to my heavenly Husband about it. Even though I have had plenty of ideas as to how I would get this ring and what it would mean to me, I never expected it the way I received it.

One day I was walking around the mall, I stopped in two jewelry stores. One had a nice band with crystals all around and it was rose gold. The second store had a few "engagement" like rings or "promise" rings in rose gold, but not what I was looking for. Honestly I did not know why I was looking for any ring. Four days later I received an unexpected monetary gift, I was blown away by the love.

This particular day I had not been to the gym, so I went to the mall to walk. It is an outdoor mall that many people go to, to walk and window shop ;). I had invited a few friends but none of them could make it. I parked my car and began my walk with Him. I came across another jewelry store, so I went inside. The minute I stepped foot in the door the lady said, "Hi, you are here for a wedding band?" I looked at her and said, "Yes, I would like to look for a rose gold band." She sat me down and showed me three rings. I loved each and every one of them. She began to ask me questions. One thing she asked was, "this has a meaning and it is not about your marriage?" I smiled and said, "Oh, yes, it is!" :) and I began to ask her if she knows God. She told me she walked away from her faith four years ago, and then she said she knows He is pulling her back because I am the 3rd person to speak to her about her faith. Then, she left to help another customer, so I took the time to speak to Him in my heart. I asked if I should purchase a ring, and if so, which one. He guided me to the middle one. When she got back she asked, "have you decided?" I said, "Yes, this one please", not even knowing the cost of the ring. She brought me to the register and told me it was on special and that she would take an additional 10% off but she had to know what this ring was symbolizing :).

I told her it is my ring from my Heavenly Husband, that I am His and He is mine. It's a reminder that I am never alone. She rang it up and the cost of the ring was the same as the monetary gift I had received!!!! :-)

I praised Him and thanked Him for my special ring and the opportunity to share about all He has done for me.

Today, on my left hand, ring finger, sits the most beautiful, shiny, rose gold, 12 amazing diamonds, wedding band from my Wonderful, Amazing, Protective, Providing, Comforting, Caring, Kind,

Generous, Forgiving, Loving, ALL KNOWING Husband. He is always in control and I love Him so much!!!!!

~ *Heather in Massachusetts is Minister in Training who was spared in order to help other women whose lives are also in danger due to their not letting go and trusting God to lead them to the safety of HIS arms!!!*

## "I am His and His Alone"

As I was watching the Be Encouraged Classic video 1 part 3, which is part of the RYM and Refresher courses, Erin was speaking about wedding rings. This reminded me I needed to send in this a praise report about what He did to provide me a ring!

My EH and I never used our rings much, I lost mine years ago and it was never replaced. But after coming to RMI and learning the importance of showing we aren't available to others, I began to pray and ponder buying one. I tried on several cheap ones from a department store and they weren't comfortable. After my divorce, I began seeking Him again for a ring, to show others I wasn't available, because I am His and His alone.

One evening I was passing by a jewelry store and felt an urge to go in, I dismissed it and went on with my business thinking it would be a way too expensive option. When I passed by the second time, I again felt the urge to go inside. I went in and looked, the sales lady asked what I wanted, and I simply stated that I had lost my ring. I felt a check in my heart so I then explained so she could understand that I had been recently divorced, but just wasn't available. She immediately liked the idea and was happy to show me the plain wedding bands I was looking for and they were in my budget! I tried on one and was surprised at the perfect fit, and to boot it was a "comfort band" that didn't even feel like it was on my finger! I felt Him smiling and approving :).

As I paid, I was surprised as she put it in a beautiful ring box and then in a pretty gift box and bag. I felt so special, like I was getting a gift! As I left the store grinning, I couldn't resist looking at it again. So following another urge I went down a little path walled in with flowers and palm trees and with little white lights along the way. I was suddenly in a very "romantic" area. I found a little bench tucked in amongst the flowers and sat down and took out the gift box, then opened my ring box.

The glint of the lights on the pretty silver band took my breath away, and suddenly I felt so loved. A romantic song was being piped softly over the sound system and as I put on my ring, I began to cry. I suddenly was pouring out to Him the wedding vow. I promised that I would always cherish and obey Him, and never leave Him. I felt such love in my heart, like a warm hug from Him. I got up and was so happy I felt like I was floating. I went home laughing, crying and praising Him. He gave me more than just a ring to wear it is now a symbol to me of that vow I gave Him!! And more than that, the ring was not only my vow to Him but a symbol of His love for me. He loves me and His love is not conditional, nor does it have limits!! It is on my finger always, and if I take it off to do dishes, I feel uncomfortable without it! I feel so cherished and honored to get to wear it. It is far more than what I planned for, but that's just like Him!!

Ladies, He loves each one of us more than we know, He longs for us, and cherishes us. Be Encouraged!!

*~ Christina in Mexico*

## "HE put His Ring on My Finger"

This journey just gets better EVERY DAY! My HH has done something so very wonderful for me!! Let me explain! I am Divorced, but not Single, and I am never alone :).

Over the last several weeks I've been doing some refreshing in my RMI Courses. I finished them for the first time a while ago, actually in early 2012, but over the last few months I had been sensing the Lord wanted me to do them again. Then suddenly I was given the invitation to take a "Refresher"! PTL that He led me to do this again, otherwise I would have missed something so very important!

One of my fellow Ministers recently sent in a PR about her NEW RING her HH gave her, "My New Ring". I was so happy for her while reading it and I could feel her JOY!! It was amazing ;). I didn't clue in at that moment while I was reading it, but my HH wanted to do the same for me!!!

Then last week while viewing Erin's *Be Encouraged* videos again, she said in the video, "HE WANTS TO PUT HIS RING ON YOUR FINGER". At that very moment my heart took a LEAP and I realized He was speaking directly to me!! I knew right there and then that I was going to get a NEW RING! (I'm giggling as I write this because HE IS SO WONDERFUL AND HE MAKES ME LAUGH!) I thanked Him and knew HE would buy it for me since I was flat broke!!

Oh ladies, let me tell you, He is the most Wonderful BRIDEGROOM! Embrace Him!!

So, yesterday after returning to work from my lunch break, this was so "unexpected", I had an envelope waiting for me and in it was a $300 bonus check from my employer! My heart took another LEAP! I was so overcome by His LOVE for me at that moment and just knew this was the money He provided for MY NEW RING!! I left work that day and headed straight to the jewelry store with My Husband leading me!

Now placed on my ring finger is a brand-new White Gold Wedding Band with 11 Beautiful Diamonds :))). The cost of my beautiful ring *and* the purchase of the *LIFETIME WARRANTY* with it was just under $300, then He bought me a nice dinner :)!! He is so SWEET!

I am HIS BRIDE and He is my BRIDEGROOM!!!

*~ Joan in Canada*

# Chapter 14

# Your Wonderful Counselor

*"And His name will be called
Wonderful Counselor,
Mighty God,
Eternal Father,
Prince of Peace."*
*—Isaiah 9:6*

There is no doubt that people who know about your situation are advising you to get a good Christian lawyer to protect you, your assets, and your children. It may be a co-worker, Christian friend, a counselor, your parents or sibling, or sadly, it could even be your own pastor.

When my husband was divorcing me the first time, I got this same advice from all the well-meaning people in my life—but **praise God** I found the "Mighty Counselor" when I came to RMI! This is what I found in my Bible when I was searching for more of what **God** had to say on the subject of any kind of litigation (divorce, restraining orders—any and all *legal* matters).

I found in His Word that He had promised to protect and defend me—why didn't any of the Christians in my life, especially our senior pastor tell me or remind me of that? Nevertheless, when I read this promise over and over again in my Bible, the decision was easy— I chose the Mighty Counselor to represent and protect me, doing exactly what His Word told me to do. And God was not only faithful, but of course, He was also mightier than **any** attorney or court could be because He is GOD, and all I had to do was to I put my trust in Him **alone!**

The Lord proved so faithful the first time, it was a no-brainer when I was facing divorce again— who else but God was good enough to represent or guide me? And along with Him, I had even greater faith than before, which meant that I walked away with even greater blessings!! And let me assure you, the greater faith was not gained because I had gone through a divorce before, but first because of my clear-cut relationship with the Lord being my Husband, me being His bride, which I didn't realize the first time. Also, a lot of my strength and resolute came from the testimonies of the other women who had faced divorce! And, third, because I knew the principles like the back of my hand from going through Erin's books again and again, while writing my own account of facing divorce, again!

Dear reader, you have just what I had the second time—the truth that you are not alone. You have a Lover— His name is Jesus and He's asked you to be His bride and He promises to be the best Husband to you too! Therefore, you, too, can experience joy and blessings that were not there for those who went before you! We all built a bridge for you to walk over into the Promise Land.

"For *your* **Husband** is your Maker, Whose name is the **Lord** of hosts; and your Redeemer is the Holy One of Israel, Who is called the God of all the earth.

"'For the Lord has called you, like a wife forsaken and grieved in spirit, Even like a wife of one's youth when she is rejected,' Says your God" (Isaiah 54:4-6).

Here is another powerful testimony that has help lay the foundation to find that narrow gate. "Enter through the **narrow gate**; for the gate is wide and the way is broad that leads to destruction, and there are many who enter through it. For the **gate** is small and the way is **narrow** that leads to life, and there are few who find it" (Matthew 7:13–14).

As you read this testimony, and every other one in this book, remember that these are women just like you and me. What happened is real; it is not a television program or a movie, but the life of someone like you, your neighbor, or your friend. Keep that in the forefront of your mind when you read all the testimonies, I was given permission to use for my book.

When anyone taps into the grace and mercy of God and chooses His protection over anyone or anything else—the result is always peace!

## Peace at Last!

I left my home of ten years to live in an apartment in February, due to a court order initiated by my husband. My husband has custody of both our children, and he is the sole occupant of our house.

I was very upset. I had the materials from RYM, but my flesh was angry. I threatened to appeal the decision, but I never did. I went before God fasting and praying with the hope that He would change my husband's heart. God had other plans—I had to move out of our home, leaving involuntarily without our two children.

I cried asking, "Why me?" In the meantime, my husband told our daughter that the divorce could not be stopped. Yet, there is no divorce, and I never went to court to fight for the custody of our kids. I surrendered all to the Lord. I left with virtually no money in my account. God sent me help for my car, heating, washing machine, and plumbing, when everything went wrong after I moved out.

My life has changed for the better—spiritually, mentally, physically, and emotionally. I have lost over twenty-five kilograms [that's more than 55 lbs.] and look better than before I was married—PTL!

God spoke to me and kept me in check. I learned to seek the love of God first, and not the love of man. Praise God for transforming me! I still have a long way to go to become the woman He wants me to be. His good work will not stop until His name is glorified.

Thank you, RYM, for your ministry, and all the encouraging testimonies I read daily on your site.

~ *Jody in Pennsylvania*

The principles in this chapter (and in the entire book) are those that I have shared with countless others. Each of them found that following these simple biblical principles often turned their situation around but always **brought peace** where there once was heartache and/or war.

**Who has known the mind of the Lord?** "Oh, the depth of the riches both of the wisdom and knowledge of God! How unsearchable are His judgments and unfathomable His ways! For **who has known the mind of the Lord**, or who became His counselor?" (Rom. 11:33–34). Speak to the Lord about whatever you are facing, then **sit quietly** and allow your heart to **hear** from Him.

"'**Woe to the rebellious** children,' declares the Lord, 'who execute a plan, but not Mine, and make an alliance, but not of My Spirit, in order to add sin to sin; who proceed down to Egypt [the world's solutions and their help], without consulting Me, to take refuge in the safety of Pharaoh, and to seek shelter in the shadow of Egypt!'" (Is. 30:1–2).

Have you sought protection from your attorney or the court system? Do you trust your attorney **more** than you trust God? "Cursed is the man who trusts in mankind and makes flesh his strength."

Ultimately, by trusting in someone else will make your heart turn "away from the LORD" (Jer. 17:5).

If an attorney was really good protection, then wouldn't we see women and children protected But we don't, do we? Instead, the opposite is true, as you and I know and sadly hear all the time. And this is all due to women trusting in man's protection (courts and attorneys), rather than Christians trusting in God alone! The same is true for a man who tries to use the court system rather than trusting God.

**It shall not approach you.** "And if anyone wants to sue you and take your shirt, let him have your coat also" (Matt. 5:38–48). This principle is one that most people choose to ignore. Jesus not only said that we should **not** fight back nor defend ourselves, but we are called (if we want to be blessed) to go beyond not resisting, by giving **more** than is being taken from us!

"…not returning evil for evil or insult for insult, but giving a **blessing instead**; for you were called for the very purpose that you might *inherit* a **blessing**" (1 Pet. 3:9).

Many of the women in RMI have shared the blessings of offering an additional piece of furniture when their spouse tried to come in and take pieces that they once had fought over! In doing so, they experienced much more than that stupid piece of furniture could buy— they experience peace, and almost always, the hate wall began to fall that was once up between them and their spouse! Some led to instant reconciliation, others found it was a building block to begin rebuilding their houses on the Rock.

Women usually worry that their husbands won't take care of them. I know the first time this was a concern for me too. Both men *and* women, we worry that our spouse will take too much of what we (or our children) deserve. Dear reader, if you act like your spouse is your enemy and fight, won't he or she fight back? Isn't that what has happened in the past time and again? Isn't that what Erin said again and again?

Yet, when we choose not to fight, but choose instead a way to go the extra mile by blessing those who are hurting us (we are then promised by God Himself) that we will inherit a blessing! And the blessings given by God are far above what anyone on earth could do for us. It is like God sets us up for a blessing and what sets the blessing in motion is an enemy coming against us! When you look at your enemies in this way, you can't help but want to bless them since they are the ones who are assuring us the blessings from God being poured all over our lives! And, then, of course it also means that we never need to fear when things come against us!

Just how big is your blessing? Well generally it will be something that compares to what has been done **to** us. And, if you do it with a great and enthusiastic attitude, then you will see those blessings multiplied!

## Laws

Even though Erin covers this in her first Facing Divorce book, Erin and I agreed it was important to go over a few things again in this book. Such as, in most U.S. states you do not violate the law if you do not sign the papers, and/or you don't show up in court; you merely lose by default. Some states make you sign a waiver that you will not appear, and in some (as in the state of Colorado when I faced my first divorce) you neither had to sign the papers nor show up.

Before you are served papers, like Erin said, take time to check the laws where you live, and don't just take one person's word for it if they tell you that you "have to" do anything. I found out the laws changed between my first and second divorce, and that now I could actually go to *get* the papers from my husband's attorney that are normally *served* by a sheriff knocking on our door.

So many of RMI members send in praise reports about how their husband still pays bills and gives to them financially when the court ruled otherwise, which is what happened to me after my first divorce. One woman just wrote to RMI and said that it wasn't until her husband had a restraining order in place against her that God turned his heart, and she was able to spend time with her children due to her *blessing* her husband. Why? Because she did not retain her own attorney and when she did not try to deny the *false* accusations made against her and she chose to stay out of court—God blessed her abundantly based on the amount of her faith and trust in Him!

**Before unbelievers.** "I say this to your shame. Is it so, that there is not among you one wise man who will be able to decide between his brethren, but brother goes to law with brother, and that **before unbelievers?**" (1 Corinthians 6:5). When the church began to ignore the biblical teachings, church members also began to ignore the church's correction— like with men or women who were in adultery.

Neither Erin or I have **never** heard of a man or woman who turned from his/her sin of adultery after being *confronted* by anyone representing the church. Some temporarily changed, but in **all** cases, they returned to the other woman or other man! So please save yourself the pain and false hope, don't ask your pastor to talk to your spouse as Jackie did:

"I was just beginning to know the Lord and was receiving counseling from the pastor at our neighbor's church and had asked my husband (then having moved out and being with the OW) to come with me. He went reluctantly, which only made him *severely* angry once the pastor started to get him to admit to his sin . . ."

So sad. Instead, of trying to *do* something, allow **God** to turn and soften your husband's heart; don't try to get anyone else to try to persuade him. Erin knows this first hand when she shares:

When I was facing divorce in 1989, I heard of a woman whose husband had come home after someone "spiritual" had spoken to him. Then low and behold, I had a dear friend of the family, a real godly man who offered to speak to my husband. He even said that he and his friends "had been fasting for some reason" and I was sure this talk with my husband must have been the reason!

I was so excited—I put all my hopes in this talk. They chose to meet at my town home (my husband was actually living with the OW on the other side of town at the time), so I left and waited a reasonable amount of time before going back. When I finally returned home, I was so sure that my husband would be there waiting for me—telling me he was moving home. But instead I found a note saying that he needed time alone for a while, *away* from me (and the children). The closeness we had come to enjoy, after following God's principles for months, was gone in an instant. It was a long time before he finally began coming over again.

Dear reader, the result in putting my faith in someone else, rather than in the Lord, almost succeeded in my giving up completely. Had I done so, I would not have been blessed with more children and RMI would never be a ministry to help you or anyone else. ~ Erin

Just imagine if Erin had fallen apart and given up. You and I would never have been encouraged and most likely would never know the Lord is our true and loving Husband!

This while facing divorce, the enemy was trying his best to do all he could to discourage me. When the church was told, both my husband and I were required to attend counseling, with several of the pastors who would lay down the law regarding adultery, whereby, if not given up, would result in my husband being removed from the church as pastor! I admired our church for their no-nonsense approach, but unfortunately, my husband simply refused to go and like other pastors, was willing to lose everything due to the sin he was caught in. "His own iniquities will capture the wicked, and he will be held with the cords of his sin" (Proverbs 5:22).

As I said, I, too, was required to go to counseling, and had to really get prayed up in order not to be tripped up by what I knew would take place during the counseling session!

## Mighty Counselor

Counseling is so common when there are marriage troubles, which everyone foolishly believes is part of the solution. The truth is, as marriage counseling increased, so did divorce *and* remarriage, since this is what is often suggested by the counselor who you come to for help!

Through my involvement with RMI, I have been ministering to women for close to a decade in our church, sharing the truth with women from firsthand experience, along with hundreds of testimonies I've read that helping Erin, who confirm my total abhorrence to *all* forms of counseling. Only once did RMI have someone get in Erin's face (in an email) telling her how much counseling helped her, then just weeks later she wrote back to say that it actually cased her husband to leave her and file for custody in order to hurt her.

If forced to go, as in things like mediation or arbitration that the court/judge might *require* you to attend, go. You should never be in contempt of court. We only advise not attending when the courts allow it. Just be sure you can't simply lose by default. But often these sorts of court appointed situations are to discuss property or custody, but in all cases, these are never about ever restoration or reconciliation. Keep this in the forefront of your mind when you attend a court appointed meeting. So that if you (or the attorney you hired who you hired to fight or speak on your behalf) offends your spouse, you may get the money, or even the children (for a time), but you will more than likely severe the hope of restoration or at least extend the journey for several years! And even though children are worth "fighting for" wouldn't you rather see your children be with both of you, restored?

And as I have shared with you, giving up all you have, will give you peace and joy—and will lead you to the desires of your heart, whatever that may be!

**Rather be wronged or defrauded.** "Actually, then, it is already a defeat for you [when you go to court or seek the help of legal help], that you have lawsuits with one another. Why not rather be **wronged?** Why not rather be **defrauded?** On the contrary, you yourselves wrong and defraud, and that your brethren" (1 Corinthians 6:7–8). God says it is better that you are wronged and defrauded (cheated or tricked) than to have the courts decide or obtaining any type of legal help. This is not only in regard to divorce— it means all forms of litigation—instead, just trust the Lord! He is free and it is the only method *guaranteed* by God to work!

"Cursed is the man who trusts in mankind and makes flesh his strength. Blessed is the man who trusts in the Lord and **whose trust is the Lord** for he will be like a bush in the desert and will not see when prosperity comes, but will live in stony wastes in the wilderness, a land of salt without inhabitant."

### *On the other hand…*

"Blessed is the man who trusts in the LORD and whose trust is the LORD. For he will be like a tree planted by the water, that extends its roots by a stream and will not fear when the heat comes; but its leaves will be green, and it will not be anxious in a year of drought nor cease to yield fruit" (Jeremiah 17:5–8).

Most women that I speak to and who write to RMI, who are in the process of divorce, are still so caught up in what they'll get, how much money for support (the men for how much they will have to pay for support), and how many possessions that they want to get or the possessions they may lose. But, if you don't allow yourself to be wronged, cheated, or tricked, how will you ever see the hand of God? If you don't allow yourself to be backed up to the Red Sea, you will never see God's power of deliverance! Remember that the "cares and riches of the world is what will choke the Word and His promises!" (Matthew 13:22.) This means that if you look at the materialistic rather than on what you say your goal is, restoration, or you fail to remember what is the most important relationship, with the Lord— it will choke your promise of an abundant life from your heart and future!

In the Bible, we are told that Demas left the Apostle Paul because the cares of the world choked the Word from him. The following verse tells us how . . . "And the one on whom seed was sown among the thorns, this is the man who hears the word, and the *worry* of the world and the *deceitfulness* of **riches** choke the word, and it becomes unfruitful" (Matthew 13:22). Scripture says specifically that it was because of "worry" and because of how "riches" are so deceitful. We believe that having riches or enough money will bring us happiness, but the rich people of this world prove this is simply not true.

Therefore, don't worry about *anything*, especially money or your possessions. Trust that "our God will supply *all* your needs," even when the legal papers say that your husband doesn't have to pay child support (or *you* have to pay support for more money than you have) or when it doesn't "look" like there will be enough money for you and/or your children to even survive. Many have fallen from their faith because the Word was choked out their faith in God to provide for them, which simply will not happen **if** you put your faith and trust in God alone!

Just a couple of days ago one of RMI's ministers who has twin girls said she was tested on her trusting God to continue to provide for her. She had been divorced for quite a while but had not gone out to work so she could stay home with her girls. But things got really,

really tough when she found she was looking at bills and rent she could not pay. Everyone kept telling her that she needed to go back to work, but she chose to continue trusting the Lord, telling Him (each time she thought about it) "Lord, I am trusting you to provide for me!"

Then, one day she was led to contact her dad because she felt convicted that she hadn't spoken to him in a while. He said he was just thinking of contacting her because there was an insurance policy he cashed out and wanted *her* to have the money. It was enough for many months' living expenses!! Erin said that RMI got her tithe from it the amount just about knocked us all over! Wow!

During my first divorce the papers stated that I wouldn't get nearly enough to feed my children and myself, not even enough to survive. But God like I read, I also chose to say nothing and trust God to soften my husband's heart. And because I trusted the Lord and didn't fight, I didn't even need to ask for more money or tell my husband my dire situation. God placed it in my husband's heart to pay all of our bills until later when he was reduced to a slice of bread and so was the OW! Then, when that source dried up, God instantly kicked in and provided for us in so many other ways. On one occasion, there was cash in an envelope in my mailbox—that someone would have needed a key to get into! On another occasion, a woman told me that as she and her husband were praying, and that God told them to pay that month's rent for me. Wild, huh?

Dear reader, God will move into our lives supernaturally IF we lay our fears aside and trust Him to provide. He may lay it on someone's heart to give you money you need, or it could come from something else no one could have imagined! So don't try to think about or make something happen. The quieter you are about it, telling only the Lord, the more God moves in your situation.

This time God chose to do something so supernatural, but only after I was able to pass a huge test, which I shared earlier when I was called to pay a past-due building pledge. That time I got a check for

$10,000 just two hours later. Then, a few months later I was tested again. I had no money in any of my accounts, and the moment I saw there was no money, the Lord told me to give away the books I had purchased wholesale from RMI—books I still owed money on! I did, and that same day I got an email that at check for over $15,000 was in the mail to me!

As I mentioned earlier, my husband had me sign papers in order for him to not pay any child support. Knowing I had done the right thing, I was tested (or maybe tormented is a better word) when a lady who does Christian counseling at our church came in where I get my nails done. Yes, Jesus is such a great Husband that He will still make sure you get your nails done, or if you haven't had this treat, you may just start.

Knowing about the divorce, she proceeded to question me about a lot of things that were really none of her business; however, I believed it was a way for her (and everyone else who was listening in the salon!) to hear the testimony of how awesome God is and how blessed a women who trusts in the Lord can be.

When this woman heard that I had signed papers so that my husband would **not** have to pay child support, she began to SCREAM at me that I had no "right" to do that! That the support was for my children—not me, and on and on she went. I listened, quietly (along with all the other ladies and nail techs in the salon), but when she finally stopped I gently replied, "What you say is true, however, my ex-husband has not been able to find a job since the divorce, and besides, God is now the Father of my fatherless children and He alone can give what my children *really* **deserve**. What any man can give is limited—but God's resources are endless!!"

Though originally outraged, it was like cold water was splashed into her face, and she quietly said she had to agree. And the humiliation was turned to gratitude when again the Lord reminded me of the truth by having Him as my Husband.

Next we'd like to share Diana's testimony so that you know that God is not a respecter of people—what He has done for others, for me and Erin, He will do for you if you simply trust Him above anything and anyone else!

## I Am SO Blessed!

"I know I have submitted other praise reports that have listed what I begin to list here, but I just wanted to thank my Lord and Savior again for all he has done! I was sitting here yesterday thinking of all the blessings he has bestowed upon me. Wow, there are so very many! My husband has never given me so many gifts!!

First of all, **my husband continues to pay ALL our bills, even after the divorce.** He gave me half of his retirement, half of the sale of our house (pray that it never occurs), spousal support that was **not** required, and child support! He said that I am to use *our* account like I always have!!

He has given me so many gifts. He still has a closet full of clothes here and all of his mail is sent here. I have noticed he is more respectful of me: he opens my car door, speaks to me with respect, says he wants what I have, and that I have changed so much.

So many prayers I have prayed: for phone calls, time with him, strength, joy, peace, and unconditional love in my heart—and I have received them all! My husband bought me a new vehicle back in May, he wanted us to have a reliable car for both me and the children! He gave me a lap desk, a new computer with printer and scanner, $2,000 because he wanted me to open an account for myself, an artist's paint set with easel, on my birthday he blew up 40 balloons, put streamers in my kitchen, got me a cake and gave me a gift certificate, then took me and the children for dinner! He has taken me to lunch on various occasions, sent me and the children over the summer to Florida for five weeks for vacation, and bought the family a new 36" television! I didn't really need the TV, but I know he will like it when he comes home, so I was very appreciative of it!!

He also bought us a new cell phone for me and the children, and he says he will continue to pay it. A beautiful necklace and earrings, that I dreamt about the day he gave them to me. He gives me a hug every time before he leaves, and kind words of how wonderful he thinks I am. God is so awesome. He is blessing me so much!

I am guessing I will think of more later. I have received so many blessings, it was hard to remember them all. God is an awesome God! I want all of you to know I would give every one of the material things up for my husband to come home. I would live under a bridge if I had to for our family to be restored! All of these things are wonderful blessings, but I want all of you to know it is in our relationship with our Lord and Savior that is the most important thing. He truly does supply ALL of our needs and wants when we believe in Him and His word!

~ *Diana in Texas, divorced and blessed*

**A defeat for you.** "Actually, then it is already **a defeat for you**, that you should have lawsuits with one another. Why not rather be wronged? Why not rather be defrauded?" (1 Corinthians 6:7). This is your answer: if you go into court with your spouse out of fear or even because "you have a plan to stop the divorce" it is already a defeat for you. You may get the money, possessions, or even an audience to proclaim your love for your spouse and your desire for your marriage, but you will lose the victory! Here is another testimony to encourage you to do what is right:

# Grateful to the Lord!

After what started out as a horrible day, the Lord has ended it what I can only describe as the **best day of my life**!

I had to go to a court ordered (all divorce cases in our county with children must have *both* parents attended before a divorce will be granted) class to help your children cope with divorce.

In reality, it was a chance to bash husbands, to learn how to move on, and to learn how to start a new relationship with someone new and make it work!

It had very little to do with children and everything to do with getting us on the "right path" to recovery. It was horrible, but I know the truth and was able to stand on the truth!

After the class, we had our weekly RYM meeting here at my house. My daughter (15), who usually does not hang around for any part of it, sat through the whole meeting with us today. She ended up saying something about her dad as everyone was leaving, and after this class, it was just enough for me, and she could tell that everything was getting me down a little. My unbelieving daughter (that we have all been praying will come to Christ) looked at me and began MINISTERING to me.

My daughter explained that I was far too close to this purposed divorce to see the truth. She explained that I cannot see how close dad is to coming home and are you ready for this?

My daughter started telling me that "sin" feels good for a short time *only*, and that the Lord's blessing was not on this other relationship her dad was in and that as soon as the last cords were broken, he would be home.

My daughter explained to me that the Lord was not holding his relationship together, so it was doomed from the start. She went on to tell me that the OW is getting bitter and jealous and pointed out things she has seen in her dad to support this (that could only be seen through "spiritual eyes").

My daughter then began telling me how God was going to restore this marriage and that IT WAS GOING TO HAPPEN! My daughter is just sure that any and all pain I may have been in and all I have gone through with this season in my life will be worth it when the Lord heals my marriage for good. She told me that we will have years of happiness from the Lord's restoration! She then went on to tell me that she believes the Lord will do something big and miraculous in this pending divorce! She explained how she has seen the Lord change me. I was able to again let her know that my sins are what brought us to this place, and I was able to lift her dad up in our conversation.

I looked at my daughter and smiled and said, "You're going to become a Christian out of all this aren't you?" She looked at me, smiled, and said, "Probably!" She gave me a look like she is having her heart turned even as we were speaking!

What a Lord we serve—I am at a loss for words even as my spirit soars! If nothing else ever comes from this whole separation and purposed divorce, my daughter's salvation was more than worth it and truth be told, **I would gladly take that in exchange for even my marriage being restored**.

I am just in awe and so humbled and so grateful to the Lord. My daughter still has a way to go, but the Lord has her on the right path now, and I am ever thankful to my Lord and Savior! I have no words, only thankfulness in my heart for the Lord's work in my daughter's life! Praise Him!!

*~ Kris in Texas, separated going through a purposed divorce*

Dear RMI,

I was reading a praise report from *Kris in Texas* the other day and felt the Lord was prompting me to write a praise report I have been putting off sending it because of time (yes, I know, it is a poor excuse). I ask for everyone's forgiveness and forgiveness from my Lord and Savior for not sending it in.

I just recently read, in the October newsletter, a donation letter from Kristen in Texas. This is me, and I wanted to follow-up on all the wonderful things that have happened since that (still somewhat embarrassing) $5.00 donation I made to your ministry. I had, at that time in August, just received the initial divorce filing papers. Unfortunately, I did not get a hold of the **not getting a lawyer principle** at the time of the initial service of the papers. I had a "fired up" **free** lawyer from a state legal aid grant.

After taking my case and starting paper work, etc. they made an unprecedented decision to drop my case because of caseload. My particular lawyer fought and argued and still could not get the case re-instated. The lawyer told me this had never happened before—ever. I just felt a calm that I could not explain and felt in my soul the Lord was telling me LOUD and CLEAR that I was *not* going to need a lawyer.

Unfortunately, again, I was so new in my walk with the Lord and still did not have the RYM resources. I talked to my pastor at church, and he helped arrange for a very high-priced lawyer for me for no fee.

This lawyer was a "fighter" and actually sued my husband for legal fees after telling me I would not have to pay! I really thought the Lord had arranged for this lawyer, because it was through my pastor, and she was a "Christian lawyer." However, the Lord really got a hold of me through RYM, and I fired her and told my husband I had done so.

Through a series of events, I ended up having to fire her twice more; each time I tried hard to make sure I did it quickly out of obedience to my Lord. I must have finally done it in the right way and the right time frame because she has filed the paper work to remove herself and for the judge to sign the motion without a hearing. The lawyer filed that paperwork, and to this date, more than a year later, the judge has not seen fit to sign that order. There is confusion and paperwork problems all over this pending divorce. The Lord is so wonderful!!

I have no idea why the paperwork is being held and is such a problem, but I just praise the Lord and know that He is at work!! What a wonderful Lord we serve!! I have no idea what the Lord has in mind in this, but I know it is a miracle!! To this date **my husband still pays all the bills and covers me on his health insurance.** He also gives me spending money. A better statement would be that the Lord has blessed me so generously by my husband continuing to do all these things!!

The Lord has led me to make sure I donate ten percent of all the spending money my husband gives to me to your ministry. You will be receiving it in the regular mail in a few days. I have received as gifts or been able to order all the RYM resources now. **I watch all the videos I have every day, all day long. I had no idea how much this would benefit me and how much this would help me!**

I encourage everyone to saturate yourself with any and all of the RYM materials you can get and with the WORD!! I have met a friend through the RYM home fellowship (although I do not lead it, the group meets in my home every week), she and I spend hours poring over Scripture, using our new concordances, and using several different versions of the Bible. With all of these things in my life and my mind, there is not only very little room for the enemy to work, but when things happen, Scripture is the first thing that comes to mind! It is wonderful to be able to tell the enemy, "It is written!!"

Faith really does come from hearing and hearing from the word of God!! "So then faith cometh by hearing, and hearing by the word of God" (Rom. 10:17 KJV). I also have divided up Psalms 119 and read a portion everyday along with the Psalms and Proverbs as RYM recommends, and I added two chapters from both the New and Old Testaments daily. The Word of the Lord really is as it says in Hebrews 4:12, "For the word of God is living and active. Sharper than any double-edged sword, it penetrates even to dividing soul and spirit, joints and marrow; it judges the thoughts and attitudes of the heart."

All of these blessings came out of the obedience to send in a little $5.00 donation that I was not sure would even help anyone or the ministry, but the Lord wanted me to send it and I did. The Lord is so wonderful, and we really do go from blessing to blessing when we walk in obedience! Malachi 3:10, "Bring the *whole* **tithe** into the storehouse, that there may be food in my house. 'Test me in this,' says the LORD Almighty, 'and see if I will not throw open the floodgates of heaven and pour out so much blessing that you will not have room enough for it.'" and John 1:16, "From the fullness of his grace we have all received one blessing after another."

Thank you so much for your faithfulness to the Lord and for giving so much of yourselves to the people who seek you through your ministry. You have helped my family and me more than I could ever express. I also thank and praise the Lord for leading me here and for all He has done for me. I started this journey to restore my marriage, but I have found wonderful friends and most important THE LORD who has given me a new heart, a new life, and a new self-esteem grounded in Him rather than my marriage, others, and false idols. I do not have enough of a gift for the written word to even get close to what I feel and all that has happened. Words are truly inadequate.

*God's Blessings,*

*~ Terri in Tennessee*

P.S.

I would also like to apologize for any praise reports I sent in before I got to this place in this restoration. I cringe when I think of them. The Lord has sooo changed me! Thanks for your love and support. This ministry and all your families are in my prayers.

**No one will see the Lord.** "Pursue peace with all men, and sanctification without which **no one will see the Lord**" (Hebrews 12:14–15).

If you wish to act as the Lord acted (Jesus was totally innocent) remember that He "opened not His mouth in defense," (1 Peter 2:23). And when you are asked, it is an opportunity to bless your spouse, not defend yourself.

"Your testimonies also are my delight; they are my counselors" (Psalm 119:24). Use Caroline's testimony to counsel you, as she said:

"As we talked about money and custody issues over the course of two hours, God shut my mouth and only opened it when I had something **fabulous to say about my husband**: his integrity, his great earning capacity, his care of the children, and his responsible way of providing all of our needs and managing our money!"

Don't you want your spouse to see Jesus in you as Caroline's husband did? But most of us quench the work of the Holy Spirit when we do the things we "want to" instead of what we "ought to." Do it **God's way**—it really works!

**Put away.** "Let all bitterness and wrath and anger and clamor and slander be **put away** with all malice" (Eph. 4:31). If you have a lawyer, there is no doubt that slander and wrath will, or has, taken place. This is what divorce is all about and why people use attorneys to represent them. You must put it all away from you. You cannot control what your attorney says to your spouse or to your spouse's attorney. He or she will also advise you about legal matters, but this is a spiritual battle, not one that will be won in the flesh. And don't be deceived, it doesn't matter if you have a "Christian" attorney or not—all **"deliverance by man is in vain!"** (Ps. 108:13). You already read this in one of the previous testimonies, remember?

**Deliverance by man is in vain.** "O, give us help against the adversary, for **deliverance by man is in vain"** (Ps. 108:12–13). RMI has been sent countless testimonies of all the ways that people try to deliver themselves, only to find that even though the judge gives a judgment of a certain amount of money or protection, the courts won't make your spouse pay (or protect you from the vengeance or physical harm due to the anger caused by the divorce)!

Physical violence is increasing. Today RMI gets many questionnaires that share horror stories of husbands who have attempted to kill their wife after arguing or when they simply will not let go. There are television shows that follow this topic as it continues to rise.

There has also been a lot of media attention given to those who don't pay child support. You surely have heard stories about men who come after their wives for physical revenge—and law enforcement can't help them! Even with police protection women, ex-wives and mothers are killed by due to anger and revenge. PLEASE, allow God to turn the heart of your spouse (Prov. 21:1) rather than using the court system to get your ex to do something he doesn't want to do.

Your spouse doesn't need stricter penalties; how foolish for us to think it will help! What men and women each need is to have a new heart— a new heart that will love you and/or your children. "I will give you a **new heart** and put a **new** spirit in you; I will remove from you your **heart** of stone and give you a **heart** of flesh" (Ezekiel 36:26). And the way you help this promise of a new heart to come about is with this promise: "When a man's ways [your ways] are pleasing to the Lord, He makes even his enemies to be at peace with him" (Proverbs 16:7). All the testimonies in this book, on the RMI website, and in the *Word of Their Testimony* books, prove this is true!

Though God used my husband for my income the first time he divorced me, this time the Lord allowed me to look to HIM alone for all my financial needs. There are so many women who whine about their husbands not paying, when in fact, everything any woman gets is from the Lord. Right? You men seeking restoration often whine even louder when you are "forced" to *have* to pay a particular sum thinking you are the ones who have to work harder to pay it. How foolish since He tells us that He is the one who wants to provide, even while we sleep!

"It is vain for you to rise up early, to retire late, to eat the bread of painful labors; for He gives to His beloved even in his sleep" (Psalm 127:2).

Believing this verse wholeheartedly, the Lord chose this time to show this principle true in my life and in the lives of other women whose husband began not paying support. What was the result? These women and I found that we had MORE, not less, than before. We not only had enough, we had an abundance—most of us ended up having more than before— than before the divorce! And none of us can explain how it happened; it was simply due to trusting our new Husband.

Not only do we have more, but also when it comes to being able to give gifts to my children, for birthdays and Christmas for instance, I give much more to my children than my ex-husband does because my Source is the Lord, and His source is unlimited! It really doesn't make any sense, but it has happened time after time and speaks volumes to my children, who, by the way, are always watching.

My ex-husband, who is now remarried, is in a two-income family. In addition, his wife gets child support from her ex-husband, and my ex-husband does **not** pay child support for his children. Then, just to stack the odds (because God wants to show that nothing is impossible for Him) my ex-husband, while visiting my children while I was in Hong Kong, came to our home and destroyed the warehouse of paperback books (after I started a Christian book company to support our lost income after he left). This meant that I basically had NO INCOME at all, and yet, I continued to be the one who was constantly blessed, and as a result, was in a position to be able to bless my children!!

When you look to your husband, to the courts, or to anyone else (even trying to figure out how YOU would *make* the money you need), you will miss what the Lord *longs* to do **for** you! He is the One who gives to us even in our sleep. It is not *earned*—it is a **gift**—just like salvation to everyone who believes and longs for Him alone! We can't earn salvation, it's a free gift.

**Take refuge in the Lord.** "It is better to **take refuge in the Lord** than to trust in man" (Ps. 118:8). A lawyer is no substitute for the Lord. Can a Christian have both a lawyer and God's protection, or are they actually in opposition to one another? Here is your answer, "Cursed is the man who trusts in mankind and makes flesh his strength. Blessed is the man who trusts in the Lord and **whose trust is the Lord**" (Jeremiah 17:5–8).

We have found in the area of divorce or child custody that you can either be blessed by trusting the Lord or cursed by what you and an attorney can do by appealing to the courts and judges. You must ultimately decide. I decided the first time that I really would certainly lose if I tried to fight against my husband. I might win more money, but thankfully, I wanted the Lord more than earthly possessions—I wanted more of Him! And since gaining Him, everything else was added to me! (Matthew 6:33.)

Now, "**Cease striving** and know that I am God" (Ps. 46: 8–10). Here is another testimony to encourage you!

## Thank you, God, for all Your Wondrous Works in my Life!

How does one begin to express the complete joy and peace that comes with walking in obedience to God? Words seem inadequate and yet, with all the blessings and answers to prayer in my life, I know that I need to find a way to write about God's almightiness, His faithfulness, and His power in a praise report.

In the past five weeks, my life has completely changed. I have known such heartache, such brokenness, such sorrow, and God took all of this and made me new. The most joyous words I could ever imagine were said by my husband one evening, as he once again talked to me of his own pain and suffering caused by my contentiousness, manipulation, and lack of submission. He said, "How does one divorce the nicest person in the world? You have changed so much"!

Although my husband was in our home, he was not planning to stay, and he told me of his hate for me, that he no longer loved me, and that there was another woman who "liked him just as he was"! He wanted nothing to do with me and was pursuing divorce.

In the past five weeks, I have confessed to him of my failing, of which he has replied that "the past is in the past, and we can move forward now." He has talked to me about the importance of God in his life, and I did not try to make him think like I think or believe what I believe. Praise God, I can now listen and keep my mouth shut. This is a miracle in itself of huge proportions!

He is HAPPY when he is around me; he has told me I look beautiful when, previously, he told me I was completely unattractive to him.

He seeks my company instead of avoiding me. We have been reunited physically as one flesh even though he told me he could never make love to me again, that all his feelings for me had disappeared, and that I was no longer desirable to him.

He has completely taken over the finances in our family, after I confessed how overwhelmed and inadequate I felt in this regard. He is the head of our household now. I discuss all things with him and do not make decisions against him or without his direction.

He travels with his work, and God has answered my prayers, providing work close to home, and even delaying his next job (in the town where the OW lives), several times, giving us more time to be with one another, and more opportunity for me to submit and show him the changes God is making in me. God has given me peace of mind. God has made me able to cope with the uncertainty, because we do not discuss the OW at all, nor do I make any reference to her existence. Fortunately, I read your books and knew about winning without a word from *A Wise Woman,* Praise God!!!

After telling me that he hated our home, and dreaded spending time here, that he avoided coming home as much as possible, he has taken a new interest. In one of our many heart-wrenching conversations, I told him that I would be willing to sell our home and move to another if he was so unhappy here. He replied that he just thought he might like to enlarge the kitchen that, in fact, he didn't desire to live anywhere else; he likes the location, the house, and the neighborhood. God is working in the most incredible ways. Sometimes, I feel physically faint at the overwhelming awesomeness of it all.

I have been caring completely for my husband. He has had surgery recently, and has been ill with stomach flu, and it was a pleasure, a joy, to care for him, for all his needs. I no longer feel exhausted, resentful, or out-of-sorts. I find complete joy in caring for my husband and family, because I know that I am in obedience to God. There is no better feeling than walking with our almighty Father. I praise God and thank God that I have been made sorrowful to the point of repentance, and that he loves me so much that I am forgiven my sins and made new.

My husband has begun to do little things for me . . . carry down the laundry, make my breakfast, make me tea, grocery shop with me, come home early, ask how I slept, if I am cold, small gestures that he had not done for so many years. I no longer EXPECT these things, but rejoice that God is turning his heart from stone to flesh. He does not say he loves me yet, but he acts lovingly, he laughs, and cuddles me. But I know that God loves me completely, and His will shall be done. For our wonderful God hates divorce, as Scripture tells us, and He made me, just as he made Eve, a "suitable" helper for my husband. Thank you, God, for all your wondrous works in my life!

~ *Ginger in Louisiana, married*

## It's Not Too Late

**Nothing is impossible.** Some of you have read my Restoration Journey Novel *after* you have been part of a divorce, or maybe even have instigated it and now you regret it—believing that for you, it's hopeless due to your mistakes.

If you have been a key player in the divorce proceedings, all is not lost. Simple ask the Lord's forgiveness and then your spouse's forgiveness. Demonstrate your desire to have the family together by dropping any and all legal action or protection. Then God will be able to begin to heal the relationship right now because **"*With* God nothing is impossible"** (Matthew 19:26).

Again, if you have retained a lawyer, dismiss him or her immediately if you want the Best to defend and bless you. Then pray, "Lord, there is no one besides Thee to help us in the battle between the powerful and those who have no strength; so help us, O Lord our God, for we trust in Thee, and in Thy name have come against this, O Lord. Thou art our God; let not man prevail against Thee" (2 Chronicles 14:11).

**Harder to be won.** If you have already been through a divorce, bitterness, resentment, and extreme anger are probably what your spouse feels toward you now. Pray that God will forgive your transgressions and blot out the bad memories he/she has (Psalm 9:4-8) and replace the bad memories with good thoughts. Spend more time with the Lord than you spend doing anything else or with anyone else, which will result in your being sweeter (again, sweetness of speech adds persuasiveness) with everyone, including your ex-spouse. And if things don't get better right away, remember, "A brother offended is **harder to be won** than a strong city, and contentions are like the bars of a castle" (Proverbs 18:19).

Rather than pursuing your spouse, keep your eyes on the Lord and your heart in HIS hands. If Jesus is all you want and all you need, and you begin to hotly pursue Him, soon your ex-spouse will begin to pursue you! Just allow the change in you begin to allure your spouse. Speaking kindly and letting them know how you feel through the look in your eye, well, you know, the way you got them the first time. Or if you really want them to pursue you, once you're a woman in love with the Lord, you will become even more alluring.

## The Desires of Your Heart

At some point, like many of us who went through a divorce, and began pursuing the Lord rather than an ex-husband, you, too, may come to a place where you begin to want the Lord permanently as your Husband and you no longer want restoration or your ex-husband. Some women tell me and write to RMI they feel guilty, as I experienced myself.

For you men, it might be different. The apostle Paul wrote concerning this in First Corinthians 7:2, 7–9 "Now concerning the things about which you wrote, it is good for a man not to touch a woman. But because of *immoralities,* each man is to have his own wife…Yet I wish that all men were even as I myself am However, each man has his own gift from God, one in this manner, and another in that…if they remain even as I. But if they do not have self-control, let them marry; for it is better to marry than to burn with passion."

The first time I faced divorce, it was pretty clearly God's will for me was to seek Him for a restored marriage. And later, due to my restoration, I was blessed with more children and found RMI! Like Erin, from the time I was a little girl the desires of my heart was to have a big family just like our mothers. My restoration also resulted in finding a ministry I could be part of and help spread in my own community and church. Had I not allowed God to do what HE wanted, and restore my marriage the first time, I would not have fulfilled the call He had on my life.

This time things were totally different. This time I knew the difference between being alone with Him (those eighteen months that my husband was gone the first time) and having a husband after we were restored. Honestly, no man can compare to the kind of Husband the Lord could be to me—no one! So this time I begged the Lord *not* to restore my marriage, so that I could be His alone!!

*"My beloved is mine, and I am His… When I found Him whom my soul loves; **I held on to Him and would not let him go**…For I am lovesick." (Song of Solomon 3:2–4; 5:8).*

Was I *afraid* since I would then be what the world would see as a single mom? No.

*"There is no fear in love; but **perfect love** casts out fear…" (1 John 4:18).*

*"'For I know the **plans** that I have for you,' declares the LORD, 'plans for welfare and not for calamity to give you a **future** and a hope'" (Jeremiah 29:11).*

With my heart of wanting to be His alone, there were many more fires I would be asked to go through, waters that I was sure would drown me. But in the end, and through it all, I experienced supernatural peace and blessings too many to count.

"When you pass through the waters, I will be with you; and through the rivers, they will not overflow you. When you walk through the fire, you will not be scorched, nor will the flame burn you" (Isaiah 43:2). Am I the only one who feels this way? Here are a few testimonies that I am not alone:

With so many women experiencing the Lord and living as His bride, RMI is seeing many more women experiencing restored marriages, but also so many who are longing for when they were His bride alone.

## "It was Better for Me Then than Now"

It has been a month since I experienced a restored marriage and I have been very happy— my husband and I are so in love. It is everything and more than what my heart desired for a restored marriage. As happy as I am, there has been something missing and I know all too well what it is.... My First Husband. My heart, mind and spirit (in the busyness of work, my home, my husband, my daughter, washing, cooking and tidying) longs for, pants for, my Husband and we both want to get back what I had together: the time alone with Him, speaking to Him, hearing Him speak to me. Once you know THIS awesome HUSBAND you cannot go back.

When you SEEK HIM, He will show you as He showed me. As I read the "What Now" that was sent to me from RMI after submitting my restored marriage testimony. This is what the Lord showed me, and it is so funny, LOL, because before I came to RMI I used to pray this same scripture for my then estranged husband, desperately, feverishly—when he was living with the ow!!

Hosea 2:7 "She (I used to put he or my husband) will run after her lovers, but she won't catch them. She will search for them, but she won't find them. Then she will say, 'I'll go back to my first husband. Things were better for me than they are now."

Back then, I used to pray desperately for my husband, praying that as he ran after his lovers, he would not find them, that he would look for them and not find them. AND NOW I KNOW. These scriptures were for me, yes me!! What struck me was these words from the verses above "I will go back to my husband, it was better for me then than now"!

During my time of being divorced, looking back it was "better for me then than now", my relationship with my Husband was idyllic, I lived for Him, I spent so much time with Him. I loved Him and He loved me; it was such a special time, it was glorious, it was marvelous, and it was awesome :) :) I loved it!!!!

Ladies, I want to encourage you to enjoy your time with your Husband (while it lasts), because before you know it, if you fall in love with your HH and let go of your EH, you will be restored to your earthly husband and long for your time you once had only for Him.

I praise God for showing me how better it was for me then than now, because my attention and focus was Him and how He taught me through RMI to put Him first. "Yet I hold this against you: You have forsaken the love you had at first" (Revelation 2:4).

God is so awesome and so in tune with you when you pray, as He shows you great and unsearchable things.

Jeremiah 33:3, "Call to Me and I will answer you and show you great and unsearchable things you do not know."

So, I'm happy to run and jump into my Husband's arms, His love is amazing!!

~ *Atarah in South Africa*

## "Missing the Solitude After Restoration"

"It was good for me to be afflicted so that I might learn your decrees" (Psalm 119:71 NIV).

This scripture has become the resonating theme throughout my Restoration Journey. I never thought in all my life that I would be giving thanks to my HH for allowing affliction to come into my life. But, if it were not for my marital affliction, I would have not come to know Him as my Lord, Savior, Heavenly Husband, Protector, Provider, and Friend. I would not have learned to put my complete and total trust in Him and I most certainly would not have known the principle of tithing. Throughout this past year, I have been privileged to witness my HH move in ways unimaginable. I am privileged to have had the opportunity to trek this pilgrimage with the remarkable women of this ministry. I have learned so much and experienced such closeness with Him and was surprised the He has decided to Restore my marriage.

Yes, my dear, sweet, beloved sisters, I am restored! I thought that I would be shouting it from the rooftops, but the fact of the matter is, I now realize that I am going to miss the peaceful solitude that I shared with Him. It is such a challenging experience to move from being totally immersed in our HH to now being restored and again being a wife. This time I am totally committed to building my house on The Rock and submitting to my EH's lead. This has been such a tremendous blessing and I am so thankful that I was led to this ministry.

So, I wanted to give praise to my HH for all of you. Thank you for allowing me the privilege to witness how He is moving in your life. Thank you for sharing your struggles, praises, and breakthroughs, as well as listening while I shared mine. Thank you for your willingness to submit to His call and be humbly transparent throughout your journey.

I will continue to SG as I have yet to complete my courses, but I will submit to His guidance and follow where this journey leads. I love you all so much, and I will continue praying for you and praising our HH for you.

*~ Cierra in Kentucky*

# Chapter 15

# Moving On or Moving Forward

*"Stretch forth thy staff"*
*—Psalm 119:24*

The question many of you are asking yourself may be, "Is there life after divorce?" Absolutely! There is a wonderful life *after* divorce, as long as you keep your eyes on the Lord and seek the abundant life He has for you—with you as His bride.

Here is a note that I from one of our RMI members, who lives in Texas with her three small children.

*Dear RMI,*

*Oh, how I love Jesus. No other words can express how dear He is to my heart. I know you understand what I am saying—though many don't. Your life and weekly messages have inspired me to live the life I never thought was possible AFTER divorce!*

*~ Tina in Texas*

The abundant life is not always (probably *never* if we are honest) the life that we "think" we want. In my life, I always wanted to be just a stay-at-home mother. I wanted to live a life of obscurity. I loved to stay at home, never going out much. This is the life I tried to hold onto and begged God to have. But His abundant life, the life that you and I were created to live, and not the kind of life we probably tried to hold onto!

I was divinely created to minister to a small group of women, "for such a time as this" and due to this, I have been asked to travel around the world with ongoing invitations to come and speak. Though at a very young age I gave my life to God, and made Jesus "Lord of my life," I knew I was not my own because He had bought me with a price—He shed His blood so I could live. But though I had said He was my Lord, and obeyed each command, principle, and His leadings, I was still trying to hold onto what I *thought* would make me happy!

Then as I spiritually matured, I chose to let go of what I *thought* would make me happy, and instead held on to *Who* I **knew** would make me happy—the Lord, my new Husband. Each day, and each new year brings me (and my family) to a higher level of spiritual maturity and more joy into all our lives! And though I know I have not yet "arrived," I am at least a little farther in my life; I am finally at a place of total and complete surrender. It began with facing divorce a second time, the debt I was left, and the neediness of the women around the world (after starting in my church, then reaching out to my community), to bring me out of my comfort zone and for me to begin to live the abundant life God had for me all along!

And now it is about to be completed after I walk away with nothing but what I can hold in two suitcases and a carry-on suitcase to live in Europe. All my worldly possessions, every person I love, all my belonging—have now been given to someone else, so that I am free to allow the Lord to lead me into a life that He promised when He first showed me that there was an abundant life that He died to give me and you!

God is now giving me the desires of my heart that *He* placed there, but they are not the same as what was in my head, which I had placed there for years. And your future, the one that He puts in your heart, is so incredible that it would seem just "too good to be true" and certainly "not you!"

For the rest of my life, who knows, I may be traveling (something I always hated to do), but my heart is filled with joy that wants to overflow! My children will be miles from me (on the other side of the world), but I know that their heavenly Father is watching over them, since He is my Husband; therefore, He is their Father and is always with them. And forevermore He will always "surround us with favor" just as He has done in our lives since I first began to seek Him above all else.

"Surely goodness and lovingkindness will follow me all the days of my life, and I will dwell in the house of the LORD forever" (Psalm 23:6).

And because of my obedience by surrendering my life to the Lord, specifically by traveling when I am a simple homebody, the showers of blessings (financial and opportunities) are opening up and pouring down all over my family, my ministry to women, and on me! The same will happen with you as you surrender your life and expect blessings that He has stored up for you. "No eye has seen, no ear has heard, no mind has conceived what God has prepared for those who love him" (1 Corinthians 2:9).

## Move On

Once a divorce goes through, so many of your friends and family members will try to encourage you to "move on." Those who love us or who believe they know what everyone else is supposed to do are going to keep pressing you. So rather than setting yourself up for more pressure from well-meaning friends and loved ones, I would encourage you to "agree" with them and *move on* by developing a more intimate relationship with the Lord! You never know what He has for the two of you up ahead ☺

When asked, you don't have to be specific, but a relationship with the Lord is the only thing that will make your future bright and heal any pain or loneliness you have.

Most people today (family, friends and coworkers) believe that it is important to find "yourself," or take time for "yourself." Yet, the way to find real happiness, and joy— joy that no one can take from you, is to really discover who you are in your relationship with the Lord. To learn what a joy it is in being His bride, not just a wife to someone.

Another benefit to *agreeing* is that as long as your ex-spouse has any inclination at all that you still want him/her, and you still have not let go of your marriage, you will see your spouse *more **committed*** to the man or woman your spouse left you for! And even if that relationship ends, they will stay angry and mean towards you. And as I said earlier, if you pursue the Lord, your ex will begin to pursue you, and allure you, instead of the other way around! I know.

This happened just days after my divorce was final; actually, it really happened even before that! When I think about it, it actually started the day *after* we both had signed the papers for the divorce to go through.

My husband began telling me how beautiful I was, running errands for me, and following me around the house when he was there to visit the children. He even set up his laptop (that he can use anywhere in the house) right next to me all day!

Because of my financial situation, and because his pull (the cords that have him bound) was still very much for the AW, he was forced to move hours away, moving in with his mom (in the same state as the AW). "His own iniquities will capture the wicked, and he will be held with the **cords** of his **sin**" (Proverbs 5:22). God moved him away for a reason, and part of it was the anticipation (or should I say, dread?) of moving away from our children, and even me! Imagine that!

The day before he was to move, I was flying to speak to women in another state, and he would be gone before I got back. Knowing he would not see me again, he called later that morning to see if we could go out for lunch. I joked, "Oh, a lunch *date*?" and he said, "Yes, a date. I will come pick you up so we can have more time to talk in the car." Again, taking the offensive position, rather than cowering in a defensive position, I asked if he had something serious to "talk" to me about. He assured me, no.

However, ladies, you and I are painfully aware that most men are not on the same playing field emotionally as a woman is, and also, they are not able to "understand" how things can be painful to us. That is why the Bible admonishes men to realize this. In First Peter 3:7 it says, "You husbands in the same way, live with your wives in an *understanding way*, as with someone weaker, since she is a woman; and show her honor as a fellow heir of the grace of life, so that your prayers will not be hindered."

It is only when men live "by the spirit" and are led by Him, that they will be able to treat women with "honor as the weaker vessel, since [we] are women." For us to expect this from a man who either doesn't know the Lord or has not made Jesus truly Lord of his life (the way we have done) is simply setting ourselves up for hurt and disappointment.

So with this in mind, even though he "said" that there was nothing he seriously he needed to speak to me about, I knew to prepare myself. The Holy Spirit, too, was ahead of me since I was led to fast that morning. When he arrived, he came into my bedroom to see if I was ready, when he pulled out an envelope that I recognized right away, since he always kept it safely in the top drawer of his dresser.

It was the first letter I sent him, along with my picture he kept for 24 years.

As I mentioned previously, I again took the offensive so as not to fall apart, and said enthusiastically, "Oh, thanks! I will put these pictures in our family photo album. The children will probably like to see them some day. But I don't want the letter I sent, so since you don't want it, I will just throw it away" and I walked over to drop it into the trash. Instead of being hurt, the pain fell on him and pierced his heart, not mine. I know that he had hoped that I would save it.

My intent is *not* to hurt anyone else. My goal is to make sure I continually walk in God's perfect will and to enjoy the abundant life Jesus died to give me. When we walk in His perfect love, it casts out all fear and we experience no more tears and no more sorrow.

**Just about a week later the Lord spoke to me that for each incident there is just ONE set of hurt, one set of pain, one set of shame.** If we are willing to take the pain or shame—it is ours! But if we, by the leading of the Holy Spirit, refuse to take it, then it will fall where it needs to be in order to bring about a change in the other person: our husbands and even the OW.

The first time around, I was more than willing, to take it all!! All the shame, pain, guilt, you name it—I took it—every negative emotion. The result was my cowering in pain in my tiny townhouse, afraid to go out (lest I run into "them"). I that made me a prisoner of all those hurts! This time, praise the Lord, He has set me free!! And now my heart is to set each of you free!!!

It is not just so we can be free from the pain, but the Bible says that sinners need to experience "Godly sorrow" without regret, that leads to repentance! "For the sorrow that is according to the will of God produces a repentance without regret, leading to salvation, but the sorrow of the world produces death" (2 Corinthians 7:10).

Our goal is to work *with* God and be aware of how He does things; it is learning to understand the principles of spiritual warfare, which too many Christians have no idea how to fight correctly. It is not simply shouting at the devil; it is living the principles and spiritual laws that the universe was created by.

By the end of the lunch "date," he kept me in the car trying to build up the courage to ask me what he had really wanted to say before I left the next day. He finally had the nerve to say what he wanted to say; my ex-husband asked me if things didn't work out with the "other person" (meaning with the AW) would I ever consider marrying him again?

This means that within two weeks of the divorce being final, he had already actively begun to pursue me, but it was God's plan that he would not "overtake me."

Just the day before, I had been encouraging another restored woman with an email who was facing the same thing with her husband leaving once again, to pursue yet another woman. So I had advised her to keep telling the Lord how HE was all she wanted, HE was all she needed, and only HE could make her happy.

Since everything I'd gone through was fresh in *my* mind, I began another "dose" of this prescription myself. So much so, that I found myself in my prayer closet pleading with God to keep it "this way" **always**! That morning, I was overwhelmed with this burning desire, "Please just let it be You and me Lord, reconsider restoration! I am just so happy with You and me alone!"

So when my ex-husband asked me, without thinking (but clearly led by the Lord) I said, "No, I don't ever want to be married again." He sort of chuckled and said (since he was aware of the RMI ministry principles I taught in our church Bible studies) that I was only saying *this* because he would think I was pursuing him if I said yes. That "no" was what I needed to say, since I needed to follow the principles I taught.

I assured him, no, this is how I *really* felt; that I clearly was no good at being a wife, and when you are no good at something, you don't really enjoy it. I said that since this all happened—I had never been happier in my life, and that I wanted to instead devote myself to my children, the Lord, and my ministry wherever that took me.

My ex-husband turned away and when he turned back, there were tears in his eyes. While he was turned away, I realized that the Lord had set me up to say just what I had said, and He had set my ex-husband up to hear that the doors were all closed for him. That the only One he could turn to would be the Lord, while things (with the AW) were not working out, which he spoke to me about after that.

Honestly, though I felt a bit sorry for him, the greater emotion was that this was more amazing than anything I could have imagined would happen. I have been in awe of the Lord for years, but this was beyond anything I had ever heard or seen! It strengthened my faith and trust in God like never before, and I could see, clearly, that every promise He had given me *would* come to pass!

God created men to *seek after* a woman, and as long as there is a chase, he is happy and is in hot pursuit of her. But once a man has caught the woman, he is no longer intrigued, and will soon seek after something or someone else. As women, our eyes need to stay on the Lord. We were created with an insatiable desire for spiritual things, so our "hot pursuit" needs to be for our Lord. I am not talking about more Bible studies, seminars, books, or conferences. It is the "closet time" alone with the Lord, and spending time in His Word (His love letters to us), on date nights with Him and those special times He has planned for you.

Though spending time with a husband is nice, spending time alone with the Lord is GREAT! Just like I used to "snuggle in the morning" or "talk all night like a slumber party" with my husband when we were married, I am doing that with my new Husband now. Wow!!

And this Husband brings no sorrow or pain with it. No marriage is perfect, but some, as I know you know, are downright painful. With the Lord, there is no pain, never any!

Instead of experiencing this kind of married life, today women are chasing men to marry them and have to continue to chase them when they leave them for another relationship. My sons (before marrying) were always facing this dilemma, since the girls were always pursuing them, and that made them totally disinterested! Even the girls' mothers began pursuing our sons for their daughters. It is a dark and fallen world.

Only as we are willing to let it all go, will we see the salvation and blessings of the Lord. I pray that each of you will do all it takes to find the abundant life God has for you! Pursing the Lord with all your heart may mean restoration, it may not; but it will mean: joy, peace, and a heart that overflows with excitement when you wake up each day.

*For more information or details to encourage you that there is life after divorce, please read the next two Michele Michaels books: *Finding the Abundant Life*, and then *Living the Abundant Life* that she wrote while going *through* her divorce and what led to way beyond her wildest dreams!

## There's Much More Help and Encouragement!

RMIEW would like to help you or anyone you know to gain more of what God has to offer as we simple trust Him during the worst and the best of times!

Please visit our website EncouragingBookstore.com for books, online videos, and new Workbook Courses. Our Restoration Fellowship members are currently growing rapidly—ladies from all around the world who want more of God! We hope you will consider joining too. **RMIEW.com**

# About the Author

Michele Michaels came to Restore Ministries International when she was facing divorce. At the time she was the mother of two small boys. After reading *How God Can and Will Restore Your Marriage* and *A Wise Woman* and she began helping Erin Thiele with her books, soon after they met while each were in Orlando, Florida. Very soon after Erin visited Michele in her home in Colorado, her marriage was restored.

Almost exactly fourteen years later Michele found herself facing divorce again while helping to update and revise a small Facing Divorce booklet for her church. After returning to RMI to Refresh her mind, Michele began to realize He had planned to use this trial for much good. It was during this new chapter in her life when Michele discovered the real reason God allowed another divorce to happen again and what she had been missing: The Abundant Life.

Look for Michele's next books on EncouragingBookstore.com and also on Amazon.com: *Finding the Abundant Life, Living the Abundant Life, Breaking free from The Poverty Mentality* and *Moving Mountains* to watch how her Abundant Life unfolds as she travels with her Heavenly Husband along her Restoration Journey.

# Check what is Also Available

on EncouragingBookstore.com & Amazon.com

Scan the code below to the available books for our Abundant Life, Restored and By the Word of Their Testimony series.

Please visit our Websites where you'll also find these books as FREE Courses for both men and women.

## Want to know more how you can Live an Abundant Life?

# Restore Ministries International

## POB 830 Ozark, MO 65721 USA
## For more help
## Please visit one of our Websites:

EncouragingWomen.org

HopeAtLast.com

LoveAtLast.org

RestoreMinistries.net

Aidemaritale.com (French)

AjudaMatrimonial.com (Portuguese)

AmoreSenzaFine.com (Italian)

AyudaMatrimonial.com (Spanish)

Eeuwigdurendeliefde-nl.com (Dutch)

EvliliginiKurtar.com (Turkish)

EternalLove-jp.com (Japanese)

Pag-asa.org (Filipino)

Uiteindelikhoop.com (Afrikaans)

Zachranamanzelstva.com (Slovak)

Wiecznamilosc.com (Polish)

EncouragingMen.org.